Beginning Anew:

Transformation through the Chakras and Expressive Arts

Nancy Winternight

Epigraph Books
Rhinebeck, NY

Beginning Anew: Transformation through the Chakras and Expressive Arts Copyright © 2023 by Nancy Winternight

All rights reserved. No part of this book may be used or reproduced in any manner without the consent of the author except in critical articles or reviews. Contact the publisher for information.

ISBN 978-1-960090-46-1
Library of Congress Control Number 2023922317

Book design by Nancy Winternight

Epigraph Books
22 East Market Street, Suite 304
Rhinebeck, New York 12572
(845) 876-4861
epigraphps.com

Table of Contents

Introduction	Beginning Anew	5
Chapter 1	Beginning with the Basics	12
Chapter 2	The Modalities	16
Chapter 3	Beginning at the Root	43
Chapter 4	Creation: The Sacral Chakra	54
Chapter 5	The Power of Emotion and Will: Solar Plexus	66
Chapter 6	Center of Devotion: The Heart	76
Chapter 7	Open the Throat and Sing!	88
Chapter 8	Pure Vision: The Third Eye	95
Chapter 9	The Crown: Spirit & Connection with All That Is	104
Chapter 10	The Higher Chakras	115
Chapter 11	Manifesting a NEW Reality	119

There is a place between the physicality of structure and chaos that is enjoyment; it requires letting go.

~ The Ones

Introduction
Beginning Anew

Open, attune, align. Remember all is new in every moment.

~ The Ones

    Those of you who know me or my work know that I work intuitively. Oftentimes, information comes to me during meditation, especially when I'm tuned into the heart chakra and my Guides speak to me. They have identified themselves as The Ones, and include Archangel Michael, Archangel Metatron, and Sananda (the soul level energy of Jesus). They have very distinctive qualities, so I usually know who the energy is coming from – the team associated with Lord Michael offers gentle guidance and protection, usually including timetables. In other words, you can expect such-and-such to happen in a particular month or on a particular day. I find it very reassuring. Metatron is more forceful or direct in his approach; I'm given imagery or specific instructions – paint this, write about this. Any information I need for a project will be provided, sometimes over several meditation sessions. What I've noticed about Metatron's directives is that they are often verified by other channelers of his energy. A particular theme may come through at the same time as the one presented to me. Sananda is ever-present in my heart, a steady warmth and sense of fullness and deep connection. When I lead others in a chakra meditation and we stop in the heart to identify our personal Guide, it's always Sananda who appears to me, and usually with some encouraging, affirming indication of where my channeling or teaching work will go. What I know is that these associations are long-standing. I've been working with these entities for eons.

Since 2018 in particular, I've been instructed to paint specific images. First, there was a series of three self-portraits – me as angel, as teacher, and as artist. I am deeply spiritual, simply meaning that I have a conscious awareness of my connection with the higher self and live my life aligned with that. I have been a teacher all my life (even as a child), and my art has always been a strong part of my life. In my book, *Soul Map*[1], I describe sitting in meditation when the idea occurred to me to overlay the three painted images, and in a sudden moment of synthesis, a shamanic figure dressed in white feathers stabbed me in the breast with one instant of severe pain, which was quickly relieved. I recently shared this story with my cousin, Jennifer, who responded that there should be a fourth painting for healer, because she perceives me as also being that. Upon reflection, I realized that healing is a 3-level process: it requires a connection with spirit (the inner self or in the case of my paintings, the Angel), guidance (the Teacher), and creativity (the Artist) – healing, after all, is a creative process. The Healer appeared when the three aspects were synthesized into one simultaneous interplay. The fourth image IS the overlay.

---

[1] Nancy Winternight, *Soul Map: Channeling, Art & Self Realization*. Rhinebeck, Epigraph Books, 2023.

Subsequently, I was instructed, very clearly by Metatron, to paint a series of twelve large mandalas, or energy wheels, if you will. They were channeled images, appearing in detail in meditation with instructions on how to paint them, and related to the Merkabah, which allows one to travel to other dimensions, along with other ascension-related information. I painted the twelve images on 36" x 36" canvases, from 2020-2021. Since that time, it's become clear (and imperative) to me that I must continue with this current work on energy centers (*chakras*) and expressive arts.

In preparing for writing this, I looked at a few texts on chakras. I've been reading people's chakra energy for years, so it's not a new topic to me by any means. But what I noticed in the texts is that they usually contain identical information: what the energy center represents, and how to unblock or clear each one using color, meditation, or even specific foods (color-related). Although directed by Metatron to explore and write a text which combines expressive arts with the chakra work, I hadn't realized how necessary this is at this time. I didn't find anything like it.

Expressive arts (movement or dance, drawing and painting, singing and sound, clay work, collage, drama, and so on) have been used as a natural part of healing since civilization began. To live in balance, we move, we sing, we express the very nature of our beings through the arts. When we are out of balance, we can find healing through these modalities. As I said, healing IS a creative process, letting go of what ails us, what no longer serves us, but then rebuilding our lives in a way that supports who we are as we evolve. In fact, when we are blocked from our creativity, we develop illness, sometimes turning to substances which seem to relieve that blocked flow. Rebuilding our lives anew requires creativity. What better way to develop our innate creativity than to be creative? Expressive arts offer that opportunity, and when we combine them with a conscious thought process, or a process of re-evaluation, we have the basis for greater inner knowing. Is this working for me now? If not, why not? We can sit and think about it for eons without understanding, but when we engage in the expressive arts, the knowing comes from within. Add the subtle body's own energy to that mix, and we have a means to recreate ourselves in a dynamic way, and to rebirth ourselves aligned with the new soul energy coming in now.

It's essential to build greater self-awareness in order to heal and grow. It's part of the basic formula for change: self-awareness + support + taking action ➔ growth, development, healing. Notice there's no equal sign. Growth or development, or even healing, is not a destination. It's a continual process, a life-long process. In order to move through the formula, greater self-awareness at any particular stage of one's life is crucial; expressive arts provide this if one engages in it wholeheartedly. I can always tell which of my students will be successful in this by how committed they are to their personal process. That willingness to go within and then the follow-through, will inevitably lead to the desired outcome.

Support is tricky. In this case, support needs to unconditional, non-judgmental. If one is doing this work with others, it's important to start with the understanding that each person's work has value and is unique to that person's inner expression. We were graded and judged as children for our artistic expression by teachers, parents, and peers. It makes us wary to reveal our true selves for fear of being hurt (our art is in essence a reflection of our innermost being). Vulnerability is called for in this work, and so it must feel safe to do the work AND to share the work with others. It may require discernment if one is not working in a setting specifically for the purpose of doing this work – with whom can I share this work or this new information I have discovered about myself? I suggest forming a group or a partnership with people who agree to these terms. It means that no one may make a comment about your expression without your permission; and it means that no one may interpret your work for you – only you are allowed to do that for yourself. Only you know the meaning of your work, and interpreting another person's work for them crosses that safe boundary. Natalie Rogers, in her book, *The Creative Connection,* tells us that we must own our comments (if we have to make them): I notice, when I look at your work, it makes *me* feel...[2] You can do this work by yourself; you are your own witness. However, there is something motivating and empowering when one does this work in conjunction with others – motivating because you must show up to do the work and empowering to make statements about yourself out loud to others. You claim space in the world for yourself, for your growth. The most important thing about working in a group is that the support should be unconditional. We trust that each person has the inner capacity to figure things out on their own; it's only our job to hold safe, unintrusive space for them. We trust they will do the same for us. There's something icky about being in a group where participants cross our safe boundaries. We need to assure ourselves of feeling unjudged, without the 'gift' of others' advice.

The last part of the formula for change, taking action, deserves some comment. Often, I see people increase their self-awareness, and hear them define what it is they need to do – that clarity is part of the process. However, there is a lack of follow-through. They abandon

---

[2] Natalie Rogers, *The Creative Connection: Expressive Arts as Healing*. Palo Alto, Science & Behavior Books, 1993.

their process, either because they fear the next step, or don't believe in themselves enough to act. Clear intention is essential, but so is actually taking the action, taking the next step, perhaps despite any apprehension. Support can help.

One of the opportunities in this work is developing one's inner vision – the ability to see where one is going in one's life in order to manifest it, to create it in form. In other words, taking the vision and bringing it into reality. We can scare ourselves when the vision is large and seemingly beyond our reach. But change doesn't need to be on a grand scale; it can be broken down into smaller steps as they appear, which makes it doable. Years ago, I heard a channeler refer to the 'blue cube': you can paint one side of a blue cube red, and it's no longer a blue cube. You didn't have to change the whole thing, only a small part of it. As we learn to trust our own inner guidance, we can see this process unfold, and as my Guides have said, *unfold it will.*

This past spring, I became aware of starting a new cycle of my life – many of us on the spiritual path have been aware of the changes happening on the planet and within ourselves as our frequency rises – personally and collectively. Who we were no longer applies to who we are becoming. I knew something was on its way but didn't know what. Pulling the Unknowable rune repeatedly reinforced this inkling. All I could do was accept the fact that Something was coming and to be open to the signs of new possibilities, staying aligned with my authentic self and the energy within. When the time was right, what I needed to know would be given. At some point, it became clear to me that I'd be working on this project – integrating chakra energy with expressive arts in some form. So here I am, beginning anew, and allowing the information to come through as it will. The process of writing this book will be intuitive. It will be a combination of what I know through teaching expressive arts, my own experience of doing expressive arts and re-evaluation work, and receiving information from my intuition and my Guides (specifically, Metatron). Let the process begin. I've decided to start at the root and work my way up…the root chakra is after all the ground, where energy comes into physicality. Each chakra builds upon the next, and building a strong foundation at the root means the structure above will be steady and secure. I invite you to join me in this upward journey, this exploration of healing through the chakras and expressive arts.

I believe to the core of my being, that when we are fully functional, we have enormous capacities to manifest an amazing world. My personal role in this life is to encourage people to see they are an integral part of the whole, that their self-expression is essential to the process of transformation on a global and Universal level.

~ Nancy Winternight

Chapter 1
Beginning with Basics

We have all been judged, not just about our artwork, but about who we are and how we present ourselves in and to the world. Naturally, we've built up outer protective shells to guard the vulnerable soft spots within. But if we are to commit ourselves to an authentic process of growth and healing, then we need to allow ourselves to become vulnerable and come out from behind the shell. The more we trust our environment – who we're with, and in the case of expressive arts, who is holding safe space for us to do the work, the more honest and vulnerable we can be. Sharing specific guidelines for creating a sense of safety is crucial, and that's where we begin. Within this space, we will not judge each other, make comments about each other's work without permission, and if we do comment, we own our statements (*I notice, it makes me feel...*), never, never, *ever* projecting our interpretation on another's work. Imagine a young child who is just beginning to draw representations of their world – perhaps they've drawn a car. Their adult makes a comment, even a positive comment – I like your house. But they didn't draw a house, they drew a car. The child concludes that they must not be very good at drawing, and the next time they'll be more guarded about it, and perhaps with enough judgment down the line from teachers and peers, stop drawing altogether. Someone who has shut down their expression will not be able to develop their fullest self. There will always be that guardedness. It's always better to say, tell me about your drawing, allowing the person to explain for themselves.

Working in small groups or in pairs with the safety guidelines in place, is a good starting point. Next, we need to go back to basics, back to before we experienced our first judgment, back to early childhood. When a child first picks up a pencil or a crayon (hopefully for the parent, with a piece of paper and not a wall), there is no intention of drawing something specific. It is just an experiment: what happens when I touch this crayon to this piece of paper? What happens when I begin to move my hand? What do I notice is happening? Gradually, the child realizes they have some control over the outcome – it's an exploration. If I move my hand like this, I can do that...no representation yet, only experimentation with line, with color, and eventually with shape. That's where we need to go when we begin expressive arts, so that without judgment we can develop our own visual language. We may not know what that is yet, but we can find out.

The process of expressive arts is about connecting with our inner being, our emotional and perhaps even spiritual life. The first exercise I do with students is the emotion scribbles. I instruct them to let go of control (you can use your non-dominant hand, which gives you less control), let go of expectation or pre-conception, let go of everything you've ever learned about art – line, color, composition; just experiment and explore. Just see what happens when you allow the oil pastel to touch the paper. I play several kinds of music (instrumental is best): calm, angry, excited...and allow students three minutes to explore the whole paper to simply see what happens. I tell students to 'let the color choose you.' In other words, look at the colors – which one calls to you? It's letting your intuition make the choice. You can change colors at any time. There's no talking to each other, which distracts from an inward focus; we work in silence. Afterwards, students share their results with each other, talking about what that experience was like. They notice similarities in their work, and differences. They notice color and line, and energy. They notice how they gradually let go of expectation or concern about the result, and just let the process take over. Expressive arts are always about the process, not the product. It doesn't matter what the end result is. Letting go of control is key, letting the energy flow through the hand, through the oil pastel in this case, is the focus. The result is immaterial.

The next question I might ask – maybe not in the first lesson, but perhaps the next time around, is how do you *feel* the energy? Where do you *feel* the energy in your body when you're angry or anxious or embarrassed? Notice the physicality of the emotion. This allows students to note the emotion within. Every expression is based in impulse – the initial impulse that drives the emotional expression is based first physically, energetically. Where? What are its characteristics? Does my face feel hot? Is the energy churning? Do I feel agitated? How would I describe it when I have strong emotion?

Eugene Gendlin was a humanistic psychologist, a contemporary of the more renown Carl Rogers. Gendlin developed a technique called "focusing" after noticing that his clients who were successful in creating change in therapy were automatically gauging their emotional experience against their verbal expression.[3] Focusing included what he saw as a six-step process: clearing some space in your mind with eyes closed; scanning the body for what he called a 'felt sense' of the experience or issue – you may locate an area in your body, probably somewhere in the torso, that feels more concentrated or perhaps heavy (he

---
[3] Eugene Gendlin, *Focusing*. New York, Bantam Books, 1978.

hesitated to put words in his clients' mouths, preferring that they developed their own description of the felt sense); giving the felt sense a name – label it; then, asking yourself, is this the right label?; if not, change it to match the felt sense more accurately; then, asking yourself, what's difficult or significant about this?; and finally, without analyzing, letting the answer come to you - your intuition will tell you. Some students can do this readily – they are apt at tuning into their bodies and feeling the energy. Others may need some practice. What I've experienced myself with this technique is that I can clear out the emotional energy by repeating the process…it changes each time; something is released each time the steps are performed. And I do believe that we can learn to tune into individual chakras by doing this – the location of the felt sense is usually in the throat, the heart, the solar plexus, or the sacral (abdominal) area.

Finding Meaning

The most important aspect of expressive arts is that it's up to the artist to interpret their own work. I encourage staying mindful of thoughts and feelings while they're working. No one else gets to find meaning in it but you, which you may be aware of as you're doing it, may become aware of as you're explaining it to others, or perhaps will make no sense at all. Any of these is just fine – no judgment, it's your process. Taking time after doing a piece of work to explain your experience to a partner or small group is important. You learn to make sense of it, you learn a language to describe it, and you take up space to value your expression. Sharing with others is sacred space – we honor each other's expressions with deep respect.

Chapter 2
The Modalities

List of Materials

A box of oil pastels, 16-24 pieces

A box of soft chalk pastels

1 set of acrylic paints – an assortment of colors (red, yellow, green, blue, violet, brown, white, and black – anything else can be mixed)

1 plastic palette or plate for mixing paint

A jar or container for water

1-2 brushes, ½ to 1 inch

1 pad of 18" x 24" *white* drawing paper, 60 lb. weight (thickness of paper)

Clay

Glue stick

Scissors

An assortment of magazines (Ask friends/neighbors/doctors' offices).

A notebook for journaling

There are many ways of doing expressive arts – I always start with the scribbles because it's fairly easy to get back to a childlike mindset without too much worry about what anyone else is going to think, or even what we're going to think about it ourselves. It's only scribbling, after all, right? Believe me, it takes time to work through the inhibitions, but trust that you'll get there. Here are some of the modalities that are available to you, or perhaps you'll think of something else altogether. I do encourage students to stick with the scribbling, unless of course something representational emerges naturally, but it's easier to focus on the emotion when we can stay away from making pictures of things.

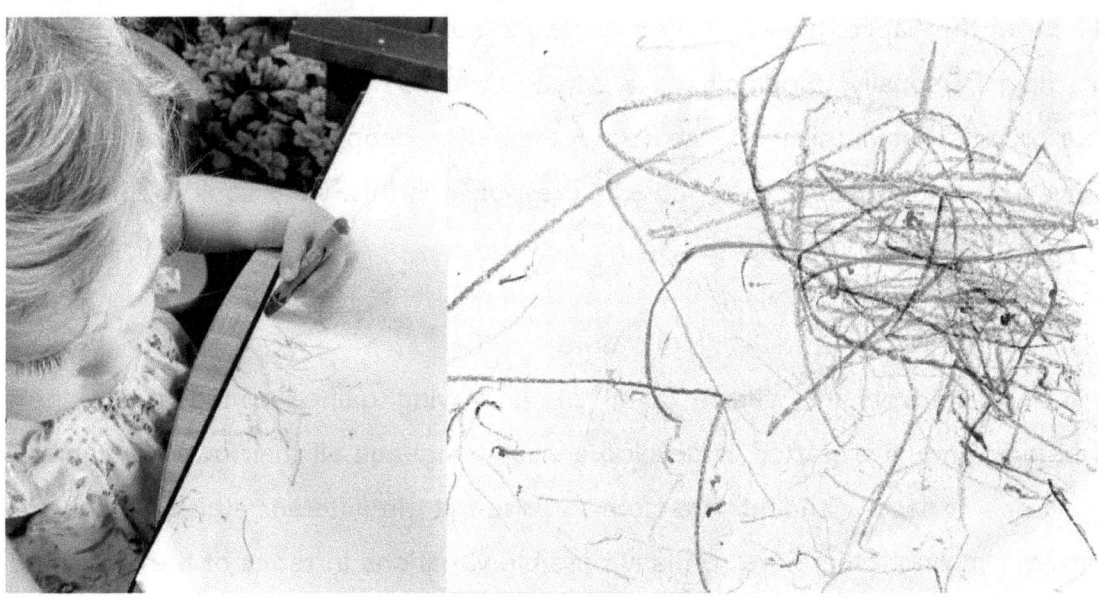

Left: 22-month-old Nova scribbles   Right: Nova's scribbles at 21 months

Scribbling with oil pastels

I've already discussed scribbling with oil pastel in the previous section, so be sure to read that first! We always start by using oil pastels. They're not intimidating and are much like the crayons we used as kids. Keep in mind that we're approaching the materials as child's play, exploration, and experimentation. The product or outcome is never the important thing – be mindful of your *process* as it unfolds. The larger your paper, the better. In class, we use 18" x 24" white drawing paper (at least 60 lb weight – that refers to the thickness of the paper). It's a big sheet of paper, so be sure to explore all of it, filling the entire thing. Personally, I wouldn't go any smaller than 16" x 20". You won't go deep enough in your process, and in this work, the deeper the better. People sometimes balk at what they perceive as 'wasting paper' to scribble. My response is this: what could be more valuable than your own self-expression?

Drawing with chalk pastels

Once students feel secure in oil pastel, having gained confidence in their own expressions, and have started to develop a visual language all their own, we can move on to chalk or soft pastel. Students are often surprised at the difference this medium can bring in ease of drawing – there are so many possible variations in terms of the actual drawing: you can draw as you would with the oil pastel, turn it on its side and use broad strokes, or even overlay colors and blend with your fingers. But to me, how readily the emotion is accessed with chalk pastel is the real magic. And this is why we don't start with it. After you've developed your language AND learned to express emotion, then you're ready to go deeper. Chalk pastel will take you there.

Lauryn blends the chalk pastel by hand.

There is one truth about chalk pastel – it's messy. Be sure to work on a surface that will catch the chalk dust (don't blow it away or dump it on the floor!). I provide a tray for students into which they can dump the dust. Sometimes sensory issues come up as well – students don't like the sound of the chalk on the paper, or the feel of it in their hands. If this is the case, at least try it again. If your resistance persists, then stick with what feels best to you. We want the work to feel pleasurable; otherwise, we won't want to do it.

More Modalities in Alphabetical Order

Attentive Listening:

Posing a few questions is another way to focus on a particular topic and is sometimes used as a warm-up exercise to an activity or series of activities. These are often done with a partner or a very small group (I think four is the maximum number of people for this activity). Each person is allowed a particular number of minutes to answer the question in the group, keeping the power equal among members. There are important guidelines for attentive listening, which keep the space safe for sharing and building trust. Here's the list of guidelines:

- **Confidentiality** is crucial for feeling safe to open up to another. Don't go blabbing about what someone has said during their turn.

- **Don't interrupt** the speaker; this is not a conversation. One person is speaking.

- **Listener:** Try not to think about what you will say when it's your turn; otherwise, you're not really listening.

- **Fill your entire time** – keep talking until the timer indicates the end of your time. You may find you go deeper this way.

- Remember, it's a **process of thinking out loud** – you don't need to know what you're going to say ahead of time.

- Don't comment on what someone has said without their permission; **we are not here to give advice**. We fully trust that the speaker has the inner wisdom to figure things out themselves. We are only holding safe space for them to do their work.

If you're working on your own, simply write the answers to your questions in journal fashion.

Clay

When I refer to clay, I mean the substance that comes from the Earth. It is earth itself – I'm not talking playdough; I'm not talking about that horrible stuff we used as kids called plasticene. I mean honest-to-goodness clay. I buy mine from a pottery supply company, though you can buy it powdered at an art supply store. Take a hunk that will fit easily into your hand (I usually cut mine into 3"x 2"x 1" pieces). Using a paper plate under it will protect your work surface. As with scribbling, we are not 'making something' out of the clay; there is no intention of creating anything representational. We'll just be with the clay and see what happens. We can push it, pound it, pull it apart, squeeze it, squish it, and smooth it. Again, no talking, just allow yourself to connect with the clay. If something starts to emerge, go with it. It's not necessarily permanent…it may shift into something else. Being earth itself, clay is very grounding. It puts us in touch with emotion very quickly. I generally put 7 minutes on the timer for clay…when the alarm sounds, I let go and step away. Let it be what it is at that moment. It can also combine nicely with other modalities…for example, contemplating what's challenging for you right now, first use clay while keeping that issue in mind, and then scribble (draw). You can follow that up with free writing to help to process it all.

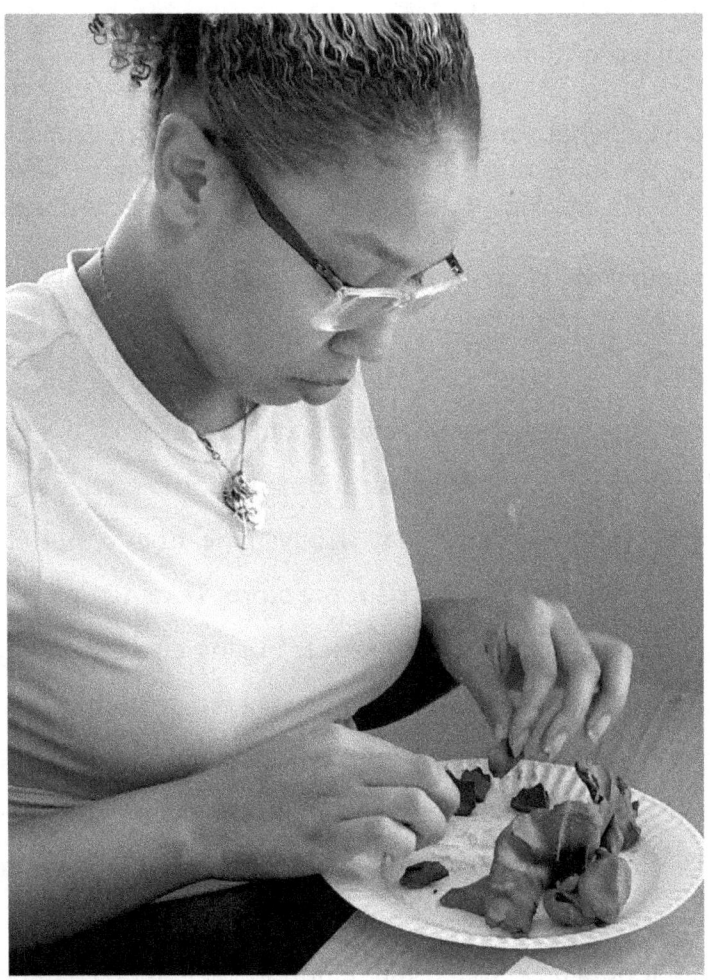

MC reflects on a current issue while manipulating the clay.

Collage

Collage is one of my favorites, and I often use it when I'm about to start a new cycle in my life. It helps me to envision where I am at the moment and where I'm going. Many people have used it to create a vision board, but it can also explore life issues. It's not as easy as it used to be to find hard copy magazines since so much is online now. But you can still find them – doctors' offices and libraries are good for that! You want to find magazines that resonate with you, so that you see yourself reflected in them. They'll give you more words, colors, and images to work with.

Again, we do collage intuitively. We're not looking for anything specific, but allowing words and images to call to us, much like 'letting the color choose you.' When words, images, or colors pop out at you from the page, cut them out. Stockpile them until you have a good quantity, rather than gluing them right away. Using a glue stick when you do attach them, will give you a smooth surface (much more satisfying than bumpy craft glue). Advice: don't use too large a surface for your collage – 9" x 12" construction paper is a good size. You can also use objects such as small boxes to add dimensionality. If you're drawn to patches of color, use them as background. I always find collages most satisfying when I've left no blank space on the surface.

Creative Movement

Ah...movement. Movement is everything – it is life itself; even our breath is movement. When we allow energy to move through our bodies, we naturally have an impulse to move. This impulse is accentuated when there's music playing. Put on some music, allow yourself to feel it, move to it, process what's going on in your life or simply move for the pleasure of it. Explore it; see what happens, much like you do when you scribble with an oil pastel. Like clay, movement is a great way to warm up to doing other modalities. Identifying a particular issue and focusing on it while you're moving, allows you deeper access to how it affects you, and how you can move through it, and release it. Continuing that awareness and flow of energy with drawing or painting deepens the process. Movement can also be used after drawing or painting – place your piece on the wall or floor where you can see it, contemplate it, and then move to it. How does it make you feel? What does it look like in movement? There's nothing (to me) more powerful for 'moving' energy than creative movement. I guarantee you'll end up in a different place, a shifted sense of how you are.

Poses are a simple, effective way of doing creative movement which require little time or space – in fact, they can be done anywhere, anytime. I will ask students to identify an issue they're experiencing (best with eyes closed) and to put their bodies into a shape or form that *feels* like that issue. I ask them to feel it from the inside out (its not about how it looks, but how it feels). I then suggest an opposite emotion – for example, how it feels when their life is in balance or things are going well, and to shift their bodies into a shape that feels like *that* – again, from the inside out. I ask them to repeat the movements – first the issue, and then its opposite. Students report to me that this simple practice allows them to be in touch with their emotions, to identify what's going on for them, and how they've invested their physical as well as emotional energy into the issue. There's often a sense of relief or release that accompanies this.

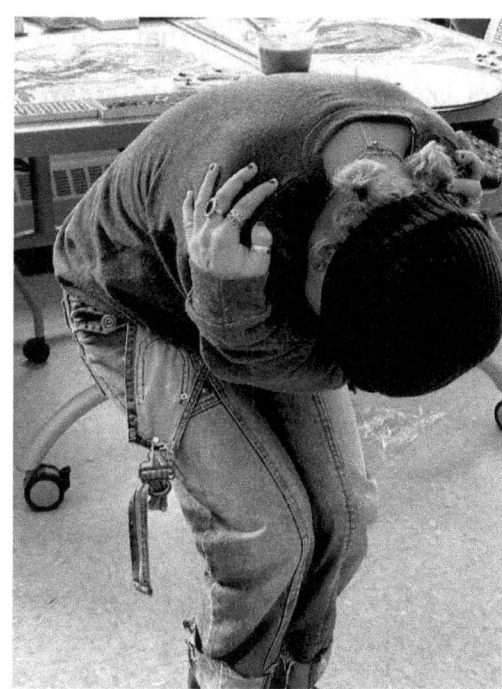 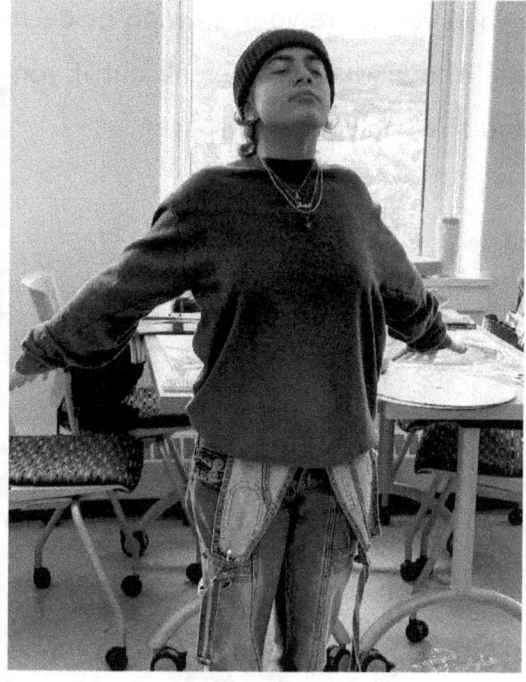

Left: Julia reflecting on an issue she's releasing   **Right:** Julia's pose for who she's becoming

Free writing

One way to process an experience is free writing afterwards. Even if you're not crazy about writing, the words will flow more easily after drawing or painting. Let go of all notions of form, punctuation, and grammar, and just let the words pour forth, much like you did in your initial scribbles. We want the most authentic expression possible, so don't stop to think about composition, the words will tell you what they want to say. Sometimes, poetry will emerge. If it does, don't worry about rhyming or number of syllables or anything you've ever learned about poetry in school. Just let the expression come. You may choose to share your writing when you share your drawing or decide to keep it to yourself. That's up to you. Be discerning about what you reveal, but if you feel like you want others to know, then go ahead and share in your safe space.

Julia free writes after drawing

Mandalas

A mandala is a sacred circle, a shape which occurs in nature and every culture on the planet. It can be used to focus our attention for meditation and is often seen outside of Hindu or Buddhist temples, constructed using chalk dust to create intricate designs. Recently, we've seen mandala coloring books, bringing the concept of the mandala into the mainstream consciousness. I see mandalas, or what I've sometimes called energy wheels, in meditation, especially the Central Sun, which is golden yellow at the center, turning a brilliant orange as it expands outward, and set in a brilliant blue background – the Central Sun is referred to as our galactic center.

In expressive arts, mandalas are again used to help focus our attention, and I feel that they are appropriate for deeper states of consciousness, especially after meditation on the heart or the crown chakras. All we have to do is trace a large circle on our paper (or just draw one, because we don't need perfection, right?). After meditation, using any medium – oil or chalk pastels, or paints, we can fill the circle with the energy we have sensed, or are sensing as we're doing the work. Again, we are not necessarily concerned about the form, except that our expression is contained within the circle. So, rather than traditional mandalas, we are creating more artistic ones. Famed psychoanalyst Carl Jung used mandalas with his patients because he believed they were windows into the soul. He used them to diagnose and for healing, and to track a patient's healing process. He used them himself as well; again, they were not what we think of as traditional, intricately designed, symmetrical mandalas, but simply artistic expressions. Every person's mandala will be different because everyone is experiencing their own, unique energy.

Students often ask me about the space on the paper surrounding the circle. I tell them it's up to them what they do with that blank space. They can leave it untouched, or they can continue their drawing/painting outside of the circle. It's their choice. Some of my favorite pieces are those where the entire paper is filled, which puts the mandala in context.

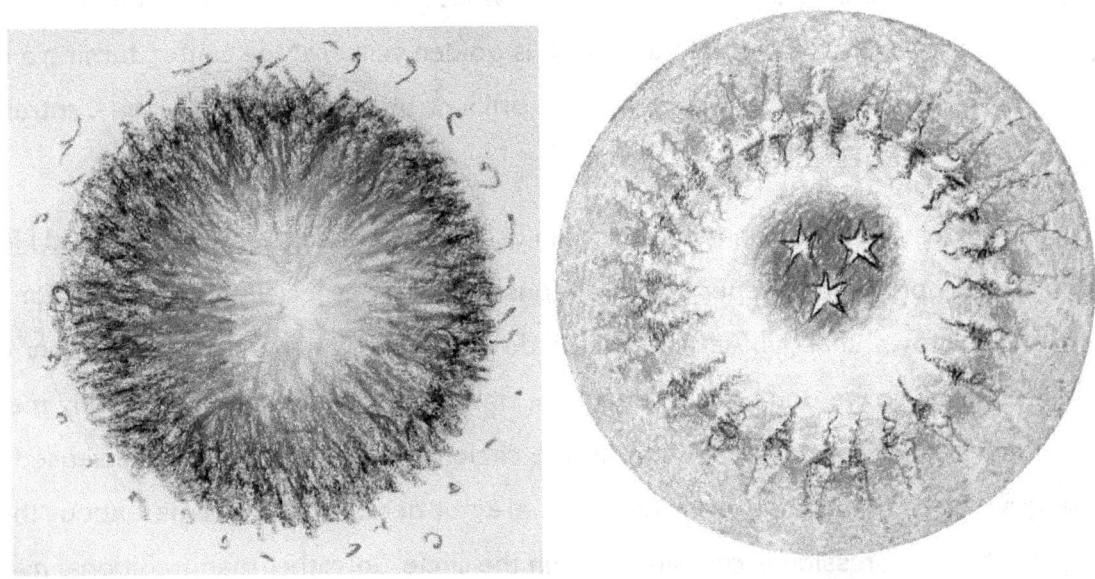

Left: *Blue Mandala* in oil pastel after meditation   Right: *Still Point* Mandala in oil pastel

Rita (left) and Mackenzie (right) create their energy mandalas.

Meditation:

My background is in Siddha Yoga meditation, which I learned from my guru, Swami Muktananda, or as we called him, Baba. We were taught to focus inwardly on the third eye, between the eyebrows, and pay attention to the spot where the inbreath meets the outbreath, and where the outbreath meets the inbreath. We were also given a choice of three mantras, which we coordinated with the breath. With practice, that spot between the breaths becomes a space, a doorway into the inner self, the nature of which is pure bliss. After many years of this ancient practice, I attest to its effectiveness. Some people's breath pauses between the inbreath and outbreath, some people the opposite. It's a natural phenomenon for the breath to pause, as you become more accustomed to this technique. We're not holding the breath – it just happens automatically with experience. Baba said we do not meditate to relax; we meditate to know the inner self.

The more I have explored my spirituality, I've come to appreciate crystals. I now hold a quartz crystal in one hand while I meditate, which acts as an amplifier of the energy. If I hold it at my third eye, it amplifies the third eye energy. If I hold it at the heart, that's what is amplified. When I was preparing to paint the first of the channeled self-portraits of my Winternight Trinity, *Gloria Caelesti*, I held it high above my head, so that it reached higher chakras, as depicted in the painting. The crystal is simply a tool that can enhance the meditation energy.

If you're interested in beginning or developing a meditation practice, I recommend doing it at the same time each day (I do it first thing in the morning), in the same place – and only use that place for meditation if you can. Sometimes using a shawl or an article of clothing that is only used for meditation is helpful. The meditation energy builds up in that one spot, in that article, so that after a while, simply sitting there will allow you to fall into a meditative state. I only use accompanying music if I am leading a meditation in class, playing the sound of Tibetan bowls in the background. The resonance seems to help guide the attention inwards.

Music

Music supports expression, especially when it is without lyrics, so that we are responding to the sound itself - the resonance, the mood, the energy frequency. By going to your favorite music platform, you can find instrumental music for most, if not all, states of being. In working with chakras, I particularly like the music which defines the HZ or Hertz – a measurement of frequency, as it relates to the specific energy centers. By doing a simple search on music platforms, you will find what you need. For example, search 'heart center HZ' or 'heart center frequency.' If searching for a mood, you can try for example, 'tense instrumental music.' If you search 'anxiety instrumental music,' you're more likely to get music which will ease the anxiety. In any case, music will usually facilitate your expression, helping to focus your attention and make the feelings you're working with more accessible. In the case of the music specifically designed for the chakras, the frequencies themselves can be healing.

Painting

Painting is probably my favorite. I use acrylic paint, though watercolors can be used for a lighter approach. There's a fluidity to painting that is missing in the drawing media.

There's a pleasure in mixing the colors on the palette, and a flow when the brush hits the paper. There can be a bit of a learning curve in terms of color mixing and adding just enough water for the paint to flow on the paper, but there's nothing more satisfying for me than the process of painting.

Sound and Movement

Okay, so let's imagine you've just done a session of either talking about your personal issue(s), or you've done a series of expressive arts modalities. You want to release the energy, clear the inner space, if you will. Close your eyes…tune in…feel the energy…and release in an authentic sound and movement. It might take two seconds; it might take a minute. It's up to you. This is not a cerebral exercise (what should I do?); it comes from the gut…tune in and just let it go. When we do this in a large group, we can do it simultaneously on the count of three. In a smaller group, we can take turns, holding space for each group member and honoring their expression. Or we can simply do it in private. You can do it whenever, wherever… You have cleared out the energy…and now you're free to begin anew.

Toning

Toning is pure sound. You don't need to be a singer to enjoy this modality, just be willing to let go of inhibition and fully enjoy the energy. Done in a (willing) group, it is the most exquisite experience of co-creation and can be quite blissful, transporting the group to an experience of higher consciousness. But it can also be done individually – I often do it during the day when the moment seizes me.

Basically, toning is the sounding of a note, any note (much like letting the color choose you), using vowel sounds (again, let the vowels choose you or happen naturally). I use the word 'sounding' much like I would use the word 'scribbling' rather than drawing. We are not singing words here, nor do we care about composition or how we sound. You can change the note as well as change the vowel at any time…ah, ee, oo, and so on. Close your eyes (or keep a soft focus) if you're in a group. Take a deep breath and just sound… Go up and down the scale, or just use a few notes. Follow the energy of what you're feeling and your response to the group's energy. You don't need to be sounding in relation to anyone else, but as you sound, listen to the group as well. This is not a time for ego; this is a time of playing/working together as one. We are sharing this experience.

Visualization

Visualization is an abbreviated form of meditation, which we often do before an exercise, simply to focus inwards, and perhaps to identify an issue we're working with, or tune into one aspect of ourselves. It only lasts a minute or two, starting with closing the eyes and focusing on the breath in a very natural way, letting go of tension in the body, and with plenty of pauses (and *slow* instructions), we turn our attention to the work we're going to do next. It does help people to access more information than if they just jumped into an activity without preparation.

Wild writing

Wild writing takes free writing to a whole other level, and actually makes a good warm-up exercise for drawing. Pick a topic, any topic, and set your timer for ten minutes.

Then let it rip – pay absolutely NO attention to grammar, spelling, or punctuation - just WRITE. It can go surprisingly deep, veering off your original topic to what matters most, but don't have that in mind, just let the words flow. Ten minutes sounds like a lot, but you'll be surprised at how fast it goes.

The Creative Connection™ or WAVE Session

The Creative Connection is the name that Natalie Rogers gave to her process of combining expressive arts modalities, one right after the other, described in her book by the same name. The inner energy flows from one modality to the next, deepening with each experience. It's one thing to do some drawing, but if, for example, you do some movement, then some drawing, and then some free writing, by the time you get to the writing you're in the flow…there's no effort; the words just pour out of you. The meaning in your work is more apparent, the self-awareness more insightful. When I did a training with Natalie at Omega Institute, we did this for five days straight. By the end of the fifth day, the depth of the awareness was profound. It's unusual to have the opportunity to do a creative connection that extensively, but a single 3-step session can take you to a place of greater understanding and self-knowledge.

For my own purposes, I have used the term WAVE to describe these multi-layered sessions, adding questions or focuses of self-inquiry. Originally, the term came about in relation to my work with women artists, combining re-evaluation work with expressive arts. WAVE stood for 'Women Artists Visionary Experience,' but I realized it also worked for 'We

Are Very Expressive.' If you think about it, a wave has a beginning and an end, a continuous process of movement. It has its individual characteristics but is a part of the whole ocean. It cannot be separated from the whole. It has its beautiful crest, but it also has a dark and sometimes turbulent underside, which may not always be visible. Once the wave breaks upon the shore, it returns to the whole. The metaphor of the wave works in this context in so many ways.

Why do this work? And why use expressive arts?

Transformation is the name of the game. We are evolving rapidly, both individually and collectively. Some of us began this work years ago; many of us came into this Earth plane specifically to aid this planetary transformation, to act as anchors and catalysts, guides, and teachers for this mission, to raise awareness and frequency. We are ascending to higher levels of consciousness together, but each and every one of us is responsible for our own journey. Some of us have been awake for a long time, some have been waking up in the last couple of years, and some are awakening now. It doesn't matter when, it just matters that we're doing it and that we're doing it individually, for our own development and collectively, for the transformation of All.

We are, each one of us, an essential piece of the whole. This is perhaps the key to understanding the ascension process. Let's start with the pizza analogy (bear with me here). Imagine you've ordered a pizza and it's delivered to your home. You're hungry and excited to eat it, right? You open the box, and lo and behold, there are only 7 slices! There's a gap in your pizza. Where did the missing slice go? And what's your reaction?? Curious? Frustrated? Angry? How about indignant (let's develop our emotional vocabulary)?

Compassionate toward the hungry delivery person who just had to eat? Bet you hadn't felt THAT way. Now imagine we are a spaceship. I use this analogy with students in the classroom. You are the pilot of the craft, orbiting Earth, and responsible for returning yourself and the ship back to Earth. Everyone else in the room (I have 30 students in a class) represents a key aspect of the spacecraft: someone is the oxygen supply, someone is the fuel which will be necessary for the return trip, someone is ground control, someone else is the computer system, and so on. This craft cannot operate efficiently without everyone's aspect of the craft. Now, as pilot, you notice that the oxygen supply is jeopardized – the gauge reads that the level is dropping rapidly. How do you feel? Think about it. No, problem. You are well-trained for such an event, and innovative. And besides, you've got ground control to help you solve the problem, right? Uh oh, your computer system has stopped responding. You have no way to communicate with ground control. How do you feel now?... Are you panicking yet? The point of this is that each and every aspect is necessary for the operation of the craft and crucial for the mission to be successful. When one goes down, the rest go down, including you. Now, imagine that you are a member of society. You notice that some people are psychologically unable to be present and fully functional in their lives. Some people don't have the resources to live well, they can only focus on survival – forget about anything else. For whatever reason, these people are unable to fulfill their role. What happens to the society as a whole if they are holding an essential piece of the pizza pie? Let's take it one step further: if every person is holding an essential piece of the world or even Universal puzzle, what happens when our wholeness is in jeopardy?

We are ascending collectively. We need to show up. We need to heal our trauma. We need to do the emotional work to make it happen. We don't just owe it to ourselves, we owe it to each other. It's not easy. It's hard to face the shadow of our lives, the difficult parts of ourselves, the parts that get triggered and lash out, or don't show up at all. The Universe has an uncanny way of kicking us in the pants when we don't move forward in our lives, when we are ready to change, but don't. There's healing to be done. The question is, how do we achieve this most effectively? We don't have time to pussy foot around (no offense to cats). We need to get down to work.

Every emotion we feel is part of a wholeness. We love to stay in the positive emotions, don't we? I'd rather feel happy than sad, calm rather than anxious. We'll do anything to remain there and avoid the darker, more challenging side. And yet, in the avoidance, we deny our totality. Sometimes we feel the shadow side of ourselves. We get angry easily or feel embarrassed. It's important to accept that it's part of our humanity. We can't feel joy without knowing misery. The avoidance, though, isn't helpful. If anything, it exacerbates the problem. And what happens is we tend to beat ourselves up for those difficult feelings and get stuck there. Not helpful. If we can see that feeling ALL of the emotions makes us whole – and let's face it, the time of duality on this planet is over, we can realize our wholeness. Give yourself a break. Be compassionate toward yourself. Have empathy for yourself. Be patient with yourself. You're a work in progress, but you can be committed to the process of becoming more fully you.

Masaru Emoto's work on water crystals is well known. In his experiments, he attached what we would think of as negative words (hate, disgust) and positive words (love, gratitude) to jars containing water samples and after freezing the samples, examined the resulting forms. Those with positive words were lovely, symmetrical configurations; those with negative words were disfigured and quite unattractive. He tried this with music also – hard metal rock resulted in disfiguration; the water responded to classical or prayerful music with beautifully configured crystals. He also looked at the difference between clear and polluted water, and the effect positive or negative emotions had on them – positive energy had the effect of clearing the polluted water. When we consider that we are largely comprised of water (approximately 60%), we can only imagine the effects of difficult emotions on our bodies. We can't deny that we have these emotions – they are an aspect of our common human experience. But denying them can only wreak havoc on our physical and energetic systems – ignoring them will prolong their effects. Honestly, I prefer to use the adjectives 'difficult' or 'challenging' to 'negative,' which connotes that we shouldn't have them. But we DO have them. Releasing them is not enough, however. We need to perform alchemy. We need to transmute the energy into something beneficial. *That* is transformation.

The HeartMath Institute has been conducting research on the energy we exude into the atmosphere around us. If we are fuming with difficult energy, where does it go? Not only are we steeping in it, doing ourselves no good; we are filling our energy field with it, affecting those around us. By transmuting our energy, we not only benefit ourselves emotionally and psychologically, and frequency-wise, but we also benefit others. After all, we're sharing the atmosphere. The more people who are doing this heart-centered transmutational work, the more impact on our collective world. Creating peace starts with us on an individual level. We need to do the transmutational work. In her book, *Stalking Wild Psoas*[4], Liz Koch quotes Rollin McCraty of the HeartMath Institute[5]:

> As more and more individuals become increasingly self-regulated and grow in conscious awareness, the increased individual coherence in turn increases social coherence, which is reflected in increased cooperation and effective cocreative initiatives for the benefit of society and the planet. From our perspective, a shift in consciousness is necessary to achieve new levels of cooperation and collaboration in the kind of innovative problem-solving and intuitive discernment required to addressing our social, environmental, and economic problems.

We're not taught this kind of work. Emotional intelligence is a highly disregarded field, though easily introduced to our educational process. If we had the tools available to us from childhood, we would perhaps suffer less emotionally as adults. At least we'd have the means with which to examine and process our emotional lives. People have been engaging in psychotherapy for many years, and not dissing its helpfulness, I do think that just talking about the issues has its limitations. What Eugene Gendlin described in his 'focusing' technique takes the process of self-examination to an energetic level. He believed that clients who were able to identify the 'felt sense' of the issue were more successful in creating change in their lives. We need to reach THAT information – to be able to tune into

---

[4] Liz Koch, *Stalking Wild Psoas: Embodying Your Core Intelligence*. Berkeley, North Atlantic Books, 2019.
[5] Rollin McCraty, *Science of the Heart, Volume 2, Exploring the Role of the Heart in Human Performance*. Boulder Creek, HeartMath Institute, 2013.

our bodies energetically, in order to increase self-awareness and expand the possibility of creating change.

This work is sensory, based in the physicality of emotion. How does emotion *feel?* How does my body feel when I am angry, sad, happy, embarrassed, and so on? What is the impulse behind it? And where is it located? What happens to my body when I feel it? When we can locate and sense the emotion, we are on track to developing the intuitive ability that will guide us. My Guides, The Ones, explained to me that "Guidance from Above mixes with emotion to create intuition." In order to open this kind of access, we have to develop our sensory system – we have to *feel* the energy. We allow ourselves to tune into the frequency of the energetic system, like you would tune into a radio station. We sensitives know that we are impacted by others' energy output and environmental frequencies because we are vulnerable or open to the external energies through our nervous systems. It is a state of *active* or alert receptivity, open to perceiving energy. When we use that vulnerability or sensitivity internally, we have access to the information coming from not only our own higher selves, but also angelic and galactic sources.

If transformation is the name of the game, then we need to do all we can to create dynamic change in our lives. The first step in the formula for creating change is greater self-awareness, so it stands to reason that we want to implement whatever promotes that process most effectively. We want to go to a deeper level than just talking, and going within affords us the ability to explore our internal workings. Tuning inwardly, using the expressive arts modalities, especially in conjunction with each other in a creative connection™, allows a level of reflection which then leads to not only greater self-awareness, but also greater meaning-making. We see our patterns, our avoidances, our strengths, our desires, and begin to see visions of our potential, our direction, our development, and ultimately, our healing. If we go deep enough, we come to know our spirit, and beyond that, our soul – the divine aspect of our being, our higher self, and experience our connection with All That Is. Our sensory systems become attuned. It's inevitable because the pathway of expressive arts leads there. But as in any practice, it takes willingness to open and commitment to one's process.

In his recently published book, *Attunement in Expressive Arts Therapy*[6], Mitchell Kossak quotes psychologist Stephen Diamond[7]:

> By symbolizing those tendencies in us that we most fear, flee from, and hence, are obsessed or haunted by – we transmute them into helpful allies, in the form of newly liberated, life-giving psychic energy, for use in constructive activity. During this alchemical activity, we come to discover the surprising paradox that many artists perceive: That which we had previously run from and rejected turns out to be the redemptive source of vitality, creativity, and authentic spirituality.

We can begin anew at any moment – now, or now, or even now. It's our choice to let go of what no longer serves us – express it, release it; but then we have the ability as creators when our system is whole and balanced to create a new life, one that is in alignment with

---

[6] Mitchell Kossak, *Attunement in Expressive Arts Therapy: Toward an Understanding of Embodied Empathy*. Springfield, Charles C. Thomas, 2021.
[7] Stephen Diamond, *Anger, Madness & the Daimonic: The Psychological Genesis of Violence, Evil & Creativity*. Albany, SUNY Press, 1996.

our authentic selves. By examining our chakras and the energies/issues they represent, we can become That. I am That That I am.

Kloe considers what she's releasing while working in paint and oil pastel.

Chapter 3
Beginning at the Root

Let's begin at the beginning. The root chakra (energy center), or *Muladhara*, is located at the base of the spine, in the space of the perineum. It is physicality – being in the body and our connection with the Earth, representing balance, stability, security, and foundational values. When we build a house, we need a firm foundation. It's no different when we build an energetic body. Some issues that can result from a closed or clogged root chakra are insecurity, mistrust, stress, depression, and feeling stuck or unable to progress. One can feel unsafe, anxious, fearful, and ungrounded. The color associated with this chakra is red.

When I first started doing expressive arts in combination with chakra energy, I led the group of women working with me through a guided chakra meditation. Afterwards, we drew our experience from the meditation (in my classes now, we paint). I noticed that each time I did this meditation, my drawing did not include a root chakra – it contained representations of all the other energy centers by color, but I could not bring myself to put in the color red, or the root chakra itself. Instead, I would put water in the drawing at the base of the spine. I concluded that I need water to feel grounded, that I need to live near water in order to do so – and in fact, I do live near water.

Years before this I had begun painting flying figures, women hovering above the ground, which I've done for many years. I explained them as connection to spirit, how I felt in my waking state. One thing they did NOT show, was being grounded. I hadn't realized at that time that I had, apparently, been born with a right angle turn in my sacrum. I developed issues with my lower back around this same time. Upon further reflection, I realized that if my spine turned, then my root chakra wasn't located in the usual place; it would be higher. The *shushumna*, or energetic channel within the spine includes every chakra. My root chakra might not be missing altogether, but would probably be closer to my sacral chakra, doubling that chakra's energy, or mixing with it. In fact, I make it a conscious process to ground at the end of my morning meditation each day by first visualizing a connection deep within Earth (this appears to me as a wet, blackish rock), but am not able to return to 'normal' waking consciousness until I envision a quartz or clear crystal glimmering in the shallows of an aqua sea.

    Psychologist Erik Erikson labeled the first stage of human development as Trust vs. Mistrust. If an infant has their needs met consistently – the child is fed, has their diaper changed when needed, and is kept physically and emotionally safe on a regular basis by their parents or caregivers, then the child develops a sense that all is right with the world and as Erikson described, develops a sense of hopefulness. When uncomfortable, they learn to anticipate that someone will come to make them feel better. They can anticipate relief, hence the sense of hope (one might question whether this is the difference between optimists and pessimists – did pessimists receive inconsistent care?). Not only will the well-cared for child develop trust in the world around them, but trust in themselves: I know I'm going to be okay. I would offer this: if, despite this solid, stable foundation in life, something unexpected happens later on in childhood or even adulthood, which causes disruption in this consistency, they may not feel as if the world is quite so trustworthy. We say, 'the rug was pulled out from beneath them'; suddenly the world doesn't seem quite so safe. Basic trust can help us to navigate the changes because we feel that, ultimately, safety and security underlie our experience and will appear again. If we have a more pessimistic outlook, then perhaps we are thrown into a more ungrounded (and uncomfortable) state.

Buddhist Pema Chodron speaks of this in her book *When Things Fall Apart*.[8]

> We long to have some reliable, comfortable ground under our feet, but we've tried a thousand ways to hide and a thousand ways to tie up all the loose ends, and the ground just keep moving under us. Trying to get lasting security teaches us a lot, because if we never try to do it, we never notice it can't be done. Turning our minds toward the dharma speeds up the process of discovery. At every turn we realize once again that it's completely hopeless – we can't get any ground under our feet (38).

> If we're willing to give up hope that insecurity and pain can be exterminated, then we can have the courage to relax with the groundlessness of our situation. This is the first step on the path (37).

Chodron believes that meditation affords us the opportunity to explore and examine this quandary. Life is full of surprises – we need to find that place within ourselves where we feel okay despite the 'not knowing', despite the Unknown of new beginnings or change. It's the nature of life to pass through its various cycles: we create our lives, we sustain them, they begin to dissipate...those of us who feel less secure may panic and start clutching at whatever we can grab onto to avoid the change, to avoid the void before the inevitable new

---

[8] Pema Chodron, *When Things Fall Apart: Heart Advice for Difficult Times*. Boston, Shambala Publications, 1997.

cycle begins. It is, however, a chance to redefine ourselves in a new way, more in alignment with who we have become, or who we are becoming. Letting go of what was, what no longer serves us, what holds us back from moving forward, is a part of the process of rebirth – part of beginning anew. Birth can be uncomfortable, even painful, but there is the promise of its potential. We are at such a period of time now – not just individually, but collectively as well. The lives we had been living, especially before the Covid pandemic, are no longer valid. Our circumstances, our context, have changed. We are evolving into new ways of being, into new consciousness. It's time to let go, to revision, and to co-create our new world.

Okay, so let's look at the issues and how we might address them.

Attending the Root

Let's take a look at how we might address the needs of the root chakra.

- Meditation
- Scribbles
- Contemplation and writing
- Movement
- Affirmation
- Other ways

Meditation #1: The Root

A more traditional means of tuning into the energy of the root chakra would be through meditation. Begin by sitting comfortably and begin to focus on your breath. Simply create some inner space for yourself. If you are a practiced meditator, then do what you would normally do to go within. If you are new to meditation, just focus on your breathing in a very natural way. If your attention wanders, simply bring it back to your breath.

Now begin to focus on the space between the breaths – between the inbreath and the outbreath. Let that be your practice, until you begin to slip into that gap. Continue breathing, allowing the breath to be your focus, no need to control it. Let it do what it will.

Drop your attention to the root chakra at the base of the spine (or more accurately, at the perineum). Feel that energy and continue your breathing as you bring your full attention to the root. Feel yourself breathing through the root. What do you sense there? Just notice the energy, nothing more. Feel the area opening and expanding; if your attention wanders, bring it back to the root. Let go of whatever feels resistant as new energy replenishes and activates the root… When you're ready to stop, wiggle your hands and feet, bring your attention back to the room, and slowly open your eyes.

Meditation #2: Grounding

Begin the meditation in the same way as Meditation #1. Once you've drawn your attention downward to the root chakra, imagine roots descending down into the Earth. Let go of all concern as you send energy down the roots. Just let it go. Continue as long as you need to. Imagine the core of Earth, with its nurturing energy, providing all that you need. Feel protected and nourished, and deeply secure. Meditate on the energy of the Earth and your relationship to it. Feel yourself surrounded by Earth's caring protection. Now bring that energy up the roots into the root chakra. Notice the connection you have between the Earth and the root chakra. Notice how secure that feels, how stable and balanced… You always have this connection. It's always within reach. Earth is always beneath you, providing a firm foundation.

When you're finished, wiggle your hands and feet, and come back into the room, and slowly open your eyes. Thank Mother Earth for her protection, and for always being there beneath you.

Scribbles

Materials: large paper and oil pastels

Here's your introduction to expressive arts in the form of scribbling. Remember the most important aspect of this work: we are focusing on the process, not the product. It doesn't matter what the drawing actually looks like. Put your judgment aside and just play, explore, experiment. Try to *feel* the emotional energy, rather than thinking about it.

Using a whole sheet of paper, preferably 18" x 24", choose some instrumental music that might feel a bit irritating to you. I'm a big fan of Philip Glass's compositions, but it can work well for this exercise. Try *Solo Piano*, most specifically *Mad Rush*.[9]

Choose from the following words what most closely relates to what YOU feel:

    Anxious
    Nervous
    Agitated
    Worried
    Fearful

Play the music and explore the page as you bring this emotion to mind. Let the colors choose you, and change colors at any time. When you're done, you can label the paper with the appropriate emotion.

Share or free write: if you have a group, go ahead, and share what that was like for you. If you're working alone, do a bit of free writing (it doesn't matter what you say, just let the words flow freely). The thing about this work is that it can be uncomfortable. You are engaging with the very thing that makes you feel uncomfortable. If you're feeling unsettled afterwards, shake it out. Make some sound, stamp your feet. You're okay. Congratulate yourself for beginning the process.

---

[9] Philip Glass, *Solo Piano*. New York, CBS Records, 1989.

WAVE #1

Materials: large paper and oil pastels, notebook

- **Contemplation and writing, or attentive listening**

    By contemplation, I simply mean self-inquiry. Grab a notebook and consider these questions. Choose just one, the one that stands out to you. You can always return to do another one later. Think about it and begin to write. Don't worry about the form, grammar, or spelling. Just write.

    1. When do I feel most insecure? How does it feel? How does it manifest in my body? What do I do?

    2. When do I feel unstable? What happens to me? What do I do when I feel that way?

    3. When do I feel anxious? What causes me to feel this way? What does my body do? And what do I do when I feel this way?

    4. If another issue comes through for you, go with that. Explore how it makes you feel.

- **Movement and Drawing** (scribbles)

    Set up for drawing.

    Using soulful or new age instrumental music (no lyrics), stand with some space around you. If you're in a group, be sure you have your own territory where you won't bump into anyone else. Stand and listen to the music. Tune in once more to your root chakra and the issue you identified and wrote about. Allow your body to move, without thinking about form. The movement comes from the inside out. Be aware of your thoughts and feelings, and the quality of the energy, and simple move. You will know when you've finished, and if in a group, it's important to give each other time to finish.

When you're done with the movement, go ahead and begin your scribbles. I say scribbles because the focus is not on anything representational. You are simply continuing the energy you began with the movement. Let the colors choose you – when you look at your box of oil pastels, what stands out to you, calling to be used? You can change colors at any time. Just explore the energy, the thoughts and/or feelings, and fill the page. Simply see what happens. And remember, it's not about the finished product, only about being aware of the process. Again, you'll know when you're done.

- **Free writing**

Return to your notebook and free write – whatever comes through. Just let the words flow without control. If you need a writing prompt, answer this: what do you know about yourself now?

- **Affirmation**

Make a positive statement about yourself. Stand up and state it out loud. Say it again with conviction. Notice any resistance you're feeling when you say it. Repeat it as much as you need to, making any body movements necessary (foot stomping, for example) until that emotional charge is released.

WAVE #2

Materials: clay, large paper, oil pastels, notebook

- **Attentive Listening (or journal writing):** identify the issue or issues that prevent you from feeling at ease or feeling a sense of safety and well-being.
- **Clay:** without music, focusing on the issue(s) identified in the first step, spend 7 minutes contemplating it/them while working with the clay. Remember, you're not making something with the clay – this is a focus on the *process* of manipulating the clay. Just be aware of your thoughts and feelings as you squish, mold, pound, tear, smooth, or otherwise use the clay. Don't talk, though you can make sound. When the timer alerts you, leave the clay in front of you as it is.
- **Drawing:** choosing soothing instrumental music, continue the energy of the clay work. In other words, don't make a drawing of the clay; instead, use the oil pastels to extend what you were experiencing with the clay. It's just an exploration – you don't need to know what you will draw. Focus again on the process, not the product. Allow the oil pastel to express what you're feeling.
- **Movement:** continue with the same music. Place your clay AND your drawing in front of you. Contemplate them; then, allow them to move you. What is the source of the movement – where is it coming from? Move until you're finished, and then **free write**. Don't worry about content or form, just let the words flow.
- Share your experience with your group.

Channeling The Ones: *Earth Connection*

The Ones have instructed me to record a channeled message for each of the chakras. I have then transcribed the audio recording. I have not edited their transmission.

*Blessed ones, we now speak about your connection with Earth beneath. You have within you an energetic structure, yes, for as we have said, consciousness **is** sacred geometric structure. You have within you that structure which allows you to connect with the energy of Earth beneath you and provides for you the balance needed to live your lives on the planet. This is not profound, no, we understand that it is a simple fact. And yet as we rise into the root, we understand that this energetic connection to the Earth is required, you see, for the physicality of your life – for being in the body. You cannot, without that connection within Earth, exist in this body. It is what roots you here. Without it, you would simply float. It would be, in fact, very difficult for you to remain in the body without that connection. And so, we would say to you to do whatever you can to maintain that, for it will be your very vitality, whether that comes from, is derived from, a food with Earth energy within, or some form of activity which allows you to maintain that connection. So, this would be any recreational activity which allows you connection with Earth. We will allow you, then, to define what that is in your own life, but it **is** a connection with nature which provides that vitality. When you are cut off from nature, you lose that source. And so, we encourage you, then, to revitalize yourselves by seeking and maintaining the connection through nature. It is as simple as that. It may be gardening, you see? Or it may be canoeing. It may be mountain climbing. It may simply be standing upon the earth. We have a vision of the beach, you see, and the sand and the bare feet upon the beach, people lying upon the beach watching the ocean waves – such a sense of wellbeing will encompass you, you see? And that is what you would prefer to have within your existence, that sense of connection, that sense of wellbeing. And so, we would let you now go and live your lives in tune with that Earth connection. Bless you.*

Chapter 4
Creation: The Sacral Chakra

The Sacral Chakra, or *Svadhisthana,* is located about three inches below the naval and is associated with the color orange. Herein lies our creativity, our sensuality and sexuality, our reproductive ability and productivity. I think of it as a center of powerful energy - much concentrated potentiality resides here. With the strong foundation of the root below, the sacral chakra allows us the power to bring through into this world what we will. It is the center of birth and rebirth, and artistic creation, and can be associated with feelings of abundance. I always think of my spiritual teacher, Swami Muktananda, dressed in orange robes, the embodiment of the Creative, attracting myriads of artists. He taught us to stand in our own power.

The cycle of life flows continuously. First comes birth…then we must sustain our creation…eventually it dissipates, dissolves, and disappears. We enter a time of pure potentiality and then a gestational period where we conceive of the new. And the cycle continues with rebirth. This chakra is core to the process. We can, in essence, create anything from this center. The chakra is associated with water, which is not surprising. When we are fully creative, we feel 'in the flow.'

When this chakra is blocked, productivity comes to standstill. The creative energy doesn't flow. We can feel stuck in a rut. It helps to know where we are in our creative cycles, however, because it's important to honor this natural process. It's unnatural to be creative or productive all the time. After we've sustained a new venture or project or expression for some time, it's important to allow its dissolution; we can enter the re-evaluation process at that point. Yes, we can give ourselves credit for what we have accomplished – it's important to do so, but it's also a time when we can question and begin to contemplate what would work better for me. We re-enter that evolutionary stage of potentiality and gestation. Perhaps we rest while this process unfolds. But as my Guides say, *unfold it will.* And we re-enter the birth process once more. Being 'in the flow' doesn't just mean flowing creativity and expression, it also means honoring the entire cycle and all its stages. We lose sight of that and beat ourselves up when the dissolution begins, or when the re-conception begins. And just as we can attune to our creative cycle with each of its stages, taking time to rejuvenate when we need to, our daily lives need this kind of nourishment and care. If we attempt to be creative the whole day through, we can easily become ungrounded, so lost are we in the bliss or angst of creation. It's important to maintain balance. Stop, take breaks, replenish.

Artists know the creative cycle. But this chakra is not just for artists! It's for humans. It's for creating your life! Having clarity about what you want to create in your life will increase efficiency. We're actually creating our lives all the time, but we may be creating a life we do not prefer, a life without clear consciousness. I'll be talking about this more as we progress through the chakras, because it's important to understand that the chakras do not operate in isolation. An energy *system* resides within us. Just as being grounded in the root puts us on firm footing for the creativity that follows (instability and the artistic process can wreak havoc), the chakras work together and, as in a well-oiled machine, operate as a whole of well-integrated, well-maintained parts. The intention that's coming in the next chakra up – the solar plexus, also supports the productivity of the sacral center. As I've said (and will probably repeat again later), *when we are fully functional, we have enormous capacities to manifest an amazing world.* That means *every* chakra is functioning to its full potential, supporting this whole process of creation. When the sacral chakra is fully operational, there's a sense of vitality like no other.

To be honest, there's no way to strengthen creativity other than being creative, like using a muscle that hasn't been used in a long time. We were born creative – it's natural instinct to build something out of nothing, to rearrange the parts, to find order in chaos. We must engage in the creative process to notice our creativity. Here are a few ways to do that.

Strengthening our Creative Power

Meditation:

You know the routine: breathe, let the world fall away as you enter your inner sanctum. Open and attune as you focus on the space between the breaths… Bring your attention down to the sacral chakra in the abdomen. See it opening, spinning, filling with light. Release your resistance to your own creative power. Feel the power building. I am creative. Continue to breathe with this in mind. I am creative… When you're ready, come back into the body, wiggle your hands and feet. And slowly open your eyes.

Collage

Materials: magazines, scissors, paper (cardstock) or other surface, glue stick

Collect as many magazines as you can, filled with color, with pictures, with bold headlines. You want as many options as you can find. As you page through them, allow the colors, images, and words to choose you. You'll be drawn to certain ones; you'll resonate with them. The colors will appeal to you, certain images will pull your attention, and words will have specific meaning to you. Try not looking for particular things, but let them choose you, just as you do with the colors when you're scribbling. Cut as many pieces as you like and stockpile them. Don't glue anything down yet.

I find that playing music that appeals to me in the background helps me to feel centered as I do this. In class, I ask students to write their requests for popular songs on the board, and I play them. Personally, I play meditative music – it's up to you. Keep it light, though.

Once you've got enough colors, images, and words cut, you can begin to assemble your collage. As I've said before, try to use a piece of paper that you can easily cover. (9" x 12" construction paper or cardstock works well). Use your colors as backgrounds to fill space, and your words and images on top. Your collage will be more impactful if the paper is entirely covered. This is the only time I will give product-oriented advice! Once you have an idea of placement, go ahead, and start gluing. Using a glue stick will give you a smooth result. You'll know when you're finished.

Collage Variations:

Beginning anew

If you're starting a new project or a new cycle, focusing on that as you look for words/images, will bring that energy through for you. You'll notice that you choose certain messages, which reflect the values or attitude with which you're approaching this new time or provide meaning. Again, let the words/images choose you, rather than looking for specifics. Don't forget the colors!

Collage with a Specific focus

If you want to create something specific in your life like abundance or change or healing, or something specific to you at this particular time, then choose that as your focus. Approach the collage with that in mind, again letting the words/images/colors choose you. You'll be amazed at what comes through for you.

WAVE #1: Feeling the Energy

What I love most about creativity is that it can be playful. Sometimes when we're doing the serious inner, emotional work that's required for making any real change, we can get bogged down in the shadow or the weight of it all. Expressive arts allow us to use that content as subject matter, but we can keep it exploratory, and even playful. If we want to build creativity, or creative power, then we need to let go of inhibition to really go for it. We need to move through our resistances to find the underlying potential. It's like entering an inner space of pure active energy.

Materials: your choice of oil or chalk pastels, or acrylic paint, large paper (at least 18 x 24"), notebook. If this is early in your process, and you are relatively inexperienced with expressive arts, go with the oil pastels first. You are just learning to let go, returning to your childlike approach to the materials.

- **Movement**

Choose your favorite *energetic* music, something that really gets your juices flowing – you can't resist moving your body to it! Choose your favorite popular music if you want (this is one of the few instances when I'll tell you that!). Make sure you've got space to move, and just DANCE. Don't think about what is looks like, just *feel* the music. Use the entire space, just as if you're scribbling over an entire piece of paper. And use your entire body. Don't hold back.

- **Scribbling**

Continue the same energy (keep the music playing) and scribble! To make this more dynamic, stand while you're scribbling and continue to move your body. Use the entire sheet of paper. Think of it as wild scribbling – no thought or planning, no composition, just scribble the energy, letting the colors choose you. Forget the form altogether. Just *feel* the music, *feel* the energy. Fill your paper with layers of color, no holding back. You'll know when you're done (if working in a group, give everyone time to finish).

- **Free writing**

    Grab your notebook and just write…don't worry about form. Just let the words flow.

- **Share** (if you're working in a group). Remember: this is not a discussion about someone's work, it's a time for each participant to speak about their process and the meaning that person has found in their own work. Give each person equal time.

- **Sound & Movement**

    Stand and close your eyes. Tune into what you're feeling at the moment. Release it with an authentic sound and movement. If in a group, give each person a turn, holding sacred space for them with honor and respect.

WAVE #2: Working through the Inhibition

The inner critic stands guard surrounding your creativity and self-expression. It's learned from early experiences that judgment makes your soft, vulnerable self in danger of injury, so it does its job to protect you. No matter what the source of the original danger, whether it was misinterpretation of your early drawings, or negative evaluation by parents, teachers, or peers, the inner critic stands guard. If you find that you feel unsure how to begin a scribble, afraid it won't be "right," or can't stop planning it out ahead of time, then this may help. Remember, there's no correct way to do expressive arts, only your way. In order to find out what your way is, you need to engage with it as fully as you can. We don't judge...remember the guidelines. Only you can interpret your work. It's up to you to find the meaning for yourself. Perhaps you can make friends with your inner critic – ask them to step aside for now to let you experiment on your own. Or perhaps you'll need to tell them more firmly! *Get lost! I don't need you now.*

Materials: oil pastels, large drawing paper, notebook, and instrumental music (what mood are you in now?)

- Using the oil pastels, hold your hand above the paper as if you're about to start scribbling. Notice how you're feeling. Is there hesitation? What's coming up for you? Really notice your thoughts and emotion. If your inner critic had a voice, what would it be saying to you (or what IS it saying?)? Take your notebook and write down one statement that your inner critic is saying to you.

- Next, share this statement with your group or say it out loud to yourself. Chances are, it's a 'negative' or limiting belief you hold about your creativity or self-expression. Rewrite it as a positive statement – it will sound like an affirmation, though it's really a contradiction of a negative or limiting belief. For example, if you wrote, "I don't know what I'm doing!" for your limiting belief, you might change it to "I have a lot of confidence in my drawing!" Or, if you wrote, "It's going to be an ugly drawing," you might contradict it with "My art is beautiful." (Note: let me just say that we don't think of expressive arts as beautiful – that in itself is limiting because if your work is really authentic, and you are getting at the stuff you've been suppressing for a long time, it's not going to be beautiful. It might be raw. It might be disturbing. If it's real, it's probably NOT going to be beautiful. At the same time, our expression is beautiful in the sense that it's real and authentic.)

The idea is to state the opposite. Now stand and say your contradiction or affirmation. Repeat it with conviction. Stamp your foot when you say it! Say it louder. What's coming up for you? What's the emotional charge attached to this? Say it until you can believe it! "I have CONFIDENCE in my drawing." "My art is STRONG." "My work is POWERFUL." State whatever the opposite of the limiting belief is for you.

- Now, put on some powerful music (Beethoven's *Eroica* comes to mind) and scribble your heart out. Just do it! Bypass the inner critic. *I don't need you now, inner critic!* Express your affirmation through the materials. Work through the resistance. Shout through your oil pastels (letting the colors choose you)!

- When you're done, free write.

- To finish, put your drawing in front of you, and make a sound from the gut, whatever that is for you. *UHN!* You can add a movement to that, combining sound and movement.

    How do you feel now?

Going Deeper

Materials: chalk pastel on paper, notebook

- **Meditation on the sacral chakra**
  Go ahead, enter your inner meditative state. Once you feel ready, begin to focus on the sacral chakra, in the belly. Breathe through the sacral chakra. Start to notice what's happening for you. How does it feel? Do you notice any sensation or anything that comes to mind for you. Notice the energy. Take your time.

- **Chalk pastel scribbles/drawing,** using instrumental music (look for something with the resonance of the sacral chakra).
  Continue expressing the energy of your meditation, this time using chalk pastels. Don't worry about depicting anything; just focus on the energy.

- **Writing:**
  Let your sacral chakra speak. What does it want to say?

- **Title your work and share** if you're in a group.

Another option: draw or trace a large circle on your paper, meditate, then draw the energy of the sacral chakra within the circle.

Channeling the Ones: Your Creative Power

*Dear Ones, we are with you at this time. It is important to understand, and we feel that most people don't, that you have within you a creative system to manifest your world as you would prefer it to be. For the past eon people have thought that they need to assign this role to some almighty God or force outside of themselves, beyond themselves. And so, the power of prayer has been essential in allowing people to ask for what they need. However, because their belief is outside of themselves, it is a much harder task for that to manifest. But when one understands that one has this system within themselves, that each of the energy centers of the body is responsible for an aspect of manifestation, then we begin to understand that we have that power ourselves. And so, when we say to go within, we ask you then to align those energy centers, to open those energy centers, and then with clarity and intention, and yes, action, for there needs to be a follow-through, it is your responsibility to manifest what YOU prefer on the planet, not assigning that to someone else, you see. And so, you come into a state of autonomy, perhaps with a capital A, because you understand that you have this higher power within yourself. And so, in terms of creativity, we would say that it is to your best interest, in your best interest, to manifest that clarity, to create that clear intention, so that you know what it is you DO want to create, and as the channel has mentioned, that if you ask yourself, if you inquire of yourself, you see – your inner self, what it is that draws your attention, that creates your excitement, that draws you, magnetizes you, energizes you, you will know your path. Most people do know their path and yet they do not understand it is through their **own inner being** that they bring that through. And so, someone who feels lost in this world simply needs to do that inner work – not as easy as it may sound for some, you see. However, we would say that if you were to take that step toward inner work – what does that look like? Perhaps meditation, yes, perhaps some sort of exercise like chanting - many people enjoy chanting, that allows you to develop that inner focus, then you will begin to see who YOU really are and what you are really here to do. And so, if there were any magic formula for unlocking your creative power - we are in fact talking about your sacral chakra here, then it would be to create some* *meditative focus in your life, some practice which allows you to focus inwardly and then tap that inner power which is innate within you. It is again as simple as that. The effort, you see, the effort to draw your attention inwardly rather than for outward pleasure or outward gratification is the key. We would say to you that this world is changing for there are enough people now upon the planet who ARE in their efforts creating their own best reality, and then collectively, that manifests for the whole, for the good of all, you see. And so, we bid that you have a pleasurable day, yes, by checking in with your self and allowing THAT energy to manifest. Blessings.*

Creativity   Nancy Winternight

Chapter 5
The Power of Emotion and Will: Solar Plexus

Wheeeeeee....

~ Nova Rose

When I focus on the Solar Plexus chakra, just beneath the rib cage, I tune into my personal power. I am strong, I am confident, and my intention is clear. I know what I want, and I feel like I can move forward in manifesting that. Here, we find the emotions, e-motion, the driving force of our lives. Ignoring the emotions can only wreak havoc later; honoring them now can fuel our journey. It doesn't mean we have to get stuck in them. We acknowledge them, we process them, we transmute them into usable energy. The solar plexus builds upon the root and sacral chakras – I am stable and grounded; I am creative with vast powers available to me. The solar plexus or *Manipura* chakra tells us we can create anything we wish to…or will. It is our personal power that allows us to.

Now here comes intuition. When my daughter was nine, and she began doubting her decision-making (typical of girls, ages 9 -11, but that's another discussion), I taught her to put her hand on her stomach, over the solar plexus, close her eyes, and using her own inner guidance to choose what she wanted. It worked! I advise anyone who is fretting over a decision to try this. Your inner guidance is reliable. It's there to protect you, to help you, to know you. *Go with your gut,* is what people say, because it's the seat of your intuition.

When I was in the midst of my channeled energy mandalas, a message came through from my Guides, the Ones, that *Guidance from above mixes with emotion to create intuition.* Even though I'm using the word *power* to describe the energy of the solar plexus, it is not power over, which I think of as an active, dominating energy, associated with control over the situation or control over others. In this sense, there is an opening to receive information, a sensory receptivity if you will. A good mantra for this is: *I am open to receiving information*, or *I am open to receiving Guidance from the Universe.* Not only does this establish your intention, but it also allows you to become open and sensitive to what will come through for you. It's a form of attunement. It's up to you to interpret what "above" means in channeled messages. I personally believe we have guides who are available to us, who work with us. They're always there; we simply need to tune into their presence. They may be angelic guides, Archangels, spirit guides, or ascended Masters. The more I am aware of my own emotions, which is certainly aided by expressive arts, and the more I can sense the energy of the emotions within the body, the more Guidance I can receive and the stronger my intuition. Therein lies the key to self-confidence. If my intuition is clear, there is less self-doubt. I have a reliable, activated guidance system to tell me what is right for me – not what I should be doing because other people tell me it's right, which is external guidance, but what works and will work for me. This brings me into greater alignment with who I am, with my authentic or inner self. And the more aligned with my true self I am, the greater my sense of personal power and well-being: all is right with the world – my world, that is. Certainly, a fully functioning solar plexus chakra is a great advantage in the process self-fulfillment.

The best preparation one can do in opening and strengthening the solar plexus, is emotional work – learning to identify what one is feeling, expressing that through the various expressive arts modalities, and watching that energy transmute into something else. In the beginning, it's enough to simply feel and identify the emotion, to label it, and to find any meaning associated with it. The release is inherent in the expression. As we become more practiced in those aspects, then we can begin to notice the point at which the energy shifts. Again, it's all about practice – actually doing the work. But when the practice is fun, not heavy labor, we're drawn to do it. There's pleasure in it, and then relief when we can (finally) let it go. For me, there's a compelling mystery that follows…what comes next?

Let's get started.

Meditation on the Solar Plexus

Get comfortable and breathe your way into meditation. Remember to find the space between the breaths… Once you've entered that inner space, bring your attention to the solar plexus, just beneath the rib cage. Just breathe through the solar plexus, allowing it to soften and open… What's the first thing you sense? Take some time to simply be in this energy center and notice what comes through for you. When you're done, you may want to write it down so that you don't forget.

WAVE #1: Investigating the Emotions

Use this session in as many ways as you wish. There is a generality about it that will allow you to explore, release, transmute any emotion you are feeling. Come back to it multiple times in order to stay current. Let's face it, life can be triggering, and difficult emotion can be really uncomfortable. The key is to work with it as it comes up and not suppress it where it festers. All you need to do is remember that you have these tools for clearing the energy.

Materials: chalk pastels, large paper, notebook

- **Visualization**

Breathe, drop into the solar plexus, and identify what the emotion is you're feeling. Another approach would be to contemplate the event/circumstance that caused you to feel the emotion. Don't analyze. Just identify it.

- **Drawing**

Put on some instrumental music that relates to the emotion you're feeling. You'll know it when you hear it because it will resonate with you. Keep your attention on the feeling and letting the colors choose you, allow the pastels to express that emotion. Use the whole page, don't rush yourself. Spending more time allows you to really explore what's going on for you. Pay attention to thoughts and feelings. You'll know when you're done. If working in a group, give each other enough time to finish.

- **Free writing**

Allow the words to flow, continuing to release the emotion…

- **Focusing:**
    - Close your eyes and clear some inner space.
    - Scan the body for the 'felt sense' of this emotion or experience.
    - Once you locate it, name it – call it something (label it).
    - Is it the right name? Compare the felt sense to the label. If it's not correct, rename it.
    - Ask yourself: what's difficult or significant about this?
    - Without analyzing, allow the answer to come.
    - Write it down. Where was the felt sense? What was it called? What was difficult or significant about it?

- **Share if you're in a group.**
- **Question:** If this was your first-time using chalk pastels, what was different about it?

WAVE #2

Materials: clay, chalk pastels, large paper, notebook

- **Identifying the emotion.**

    As in the first creative connection, first identify the emotion (or emotions) you're addressing. Close your eyes, focus on the solar plexus. What's there for you? Or again, contemplate the experience that triggered your discomfort.

- **Clay (no music)**

    Set your timer for 7 minutes and just BE with the clay. Focus on the emotion. Remember you don't have to make anything, though if anything starts to emerge, just go with it. Change it if you want or if it takes you somewhere else. Stay mindful of thoughts and emotion. When the timer sounds, put it down.

- **Chalk pastels** (instrumental music resonating with the solar plexus)

    Contemplate your clay work and continue the energy with the chalk pastels. Fill the entire page. Don't be afraid to explore what the chalk pastels do or how the colors can blend. Don't worry about the outcome. Be aware of your thoughts and feelings.

- **Free writing**

    Continue in words. Just let the words flow.

- **Share, if you're in a group.**

WAVE #3:

Materials: Instrumental music, chalk pastels, large paper

- **Creative Movement**

    Stand up and find some space to move in. Play the instrumental music that resonates with the emotion. Close your eyes or keep a soft focus to stay aware of your territory and check in with your body. Where is the energy located? Begin to explore that energy with your body's movements – they can be small or more dramatic. Feel it from the inside out (don't worry about how it appears, only how it feels to move your body to the music and to the energy). Let your body guide you. If you're in a group, you can move on to step 2 when you're ready. Let group members have the time they need.

- **Drawing with chalk pastels** (If you find your senses do not tolerate chalk pastels, use oil pastels instead.)

    Continue the exploration of the emotion with the chalk pastels. Give yourself enough time to fully explore it. Stay mindful of thoughts and feelings.

- **Free writing** (optional)

    Continue the process with words.

- **Sound and movement**

With eyes closed, tune into your gut. Take your time to feel it. Then make an authentic sound and movement to express what you're feeling. If in a group: give each person a turn and honor their expression with the utmost respect.

- **Share** if in a group.

Going Deeper

Materials: chalk pastels or paint, large paper, notebook

As you continue the work, especially focusing on the solar plexus chakra, you may find that you're not just identifying and releasing emotion, but the energy is turning into something else. In essence, you are transmuting the energy from one form into another, as in alchemy. As you go deeper, notice that shift as it takes place. Your self-awareness is deepening now.

- **Meditation**

Breathe your way into your meditative state. Take your time to become absorbed. Now shift your attention to the solar plexus, beneath the rib cage. Breathe through the solar plexus. What do you notice? What wants to be noticed? Continue to meditate on this energy center of the body. When you're done, be sure to re-ground, wiggling your hands and feet, and become aware of the room you're in as you slowly open your eyes.

- **Movement**

  How did your solar plexus *FEEL*?? Using the same music as in WAVE #3, move to the energy you felt or are feeling. Does the energy shift or change while you're moving? Simply notice the change if it happens.

- **Chalk pastels or paint**

  Continue to explore the energy of this experience (meditation and/or movement) through your chosen medium. Again, don't worry about depicting anything specific except how the energy feels to you.

- **Writing:** Let your drawing speak. What does it want to say?
- **Share**, if you're in a group.

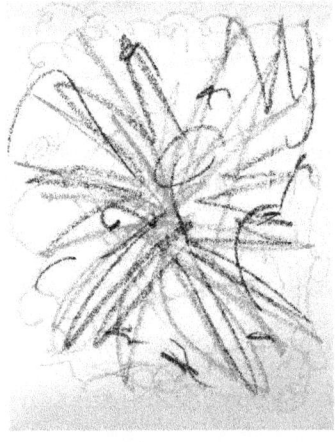
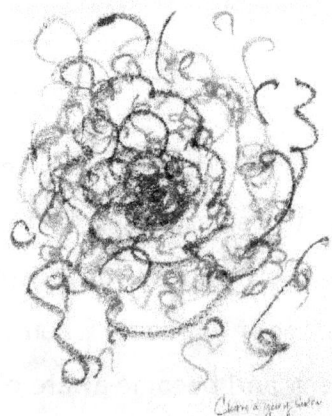
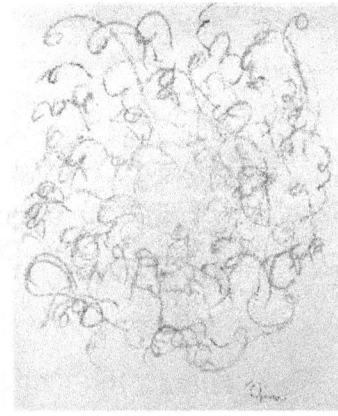

UHN! (Anger)   *Clearing a Year of Shadow*   *Openness*

Channeling the Ones: Clean and Clear Emotion

*As we focus on the solar plexus, we see that it is like a brilliant, yellow sun, with rays shooting out in all directions. For if the emotions are kept pure, if they are processed as they arise, then we keep the solar plexus free and clear to shine brightly from within. It is not that we deny the emotions, for as humans it is quite natural to respond to others, to situations, to whatever scenes or dramas arise around you and from within you. And yet we do not become **fixed** in the emotion. There is a tendency among humans to become fixed in that position, in that emotional position, and then to punish oneself for feeling that. And we would say, then, that it is more effective in your life to use the emotion to fuel your life, to see the emotion come, pass through it, acknowledge it, and to let it go. If it helps you then in releasing it to express it as the channel has mentioned, then it is to your advantage to do so. The idea here is to keep the emotion flowing... You see it is related to the water, the fluidity of energy. And when we become fixed in an emotion, it is as if you have built a dam to stop the flow. And so, that energy, that emotion, builds until it must spill over into your life, where it may wreak havoc. And so, we would say to you to find the means, as the channel does describe, to process your emotion, to become aware that you are experiencing it in the moment, and to take the time to explore it, identify it, perhaps identify the reason for it if you feel it is necessary, but then to move on...and to see it, to feel it, to experience it dissipating, dissolving, letting go...and moving on...to whatever comes next. And in this way, we keep the emotion pure; we keep the emotion flowing. And we keep the energy center clear so that it may shine brightly. For your emotional center is key in your creative process. It lends power, it lends energy, fuel, you see, for that creative machine. Yes, referring to this center and this system as a machine may seem rather cold, detached; however, what we imply is that these chakras work together as if they are a technological entity unto itself, will we say, that creates what it is you wish. And so, we say we need the fuel, the clean and clear fuel which burns without exhaust, yes, without exhaustion, and keeps your process of growth, of upliftment, of expression, flowing. Ah, so, we would say to you to go in peace and many blessings.*

Chapter 6
Center of Devotion: The Heart

Ah, the heart. There is a Merkabah that surrounds the body – we usually represent this as a triangle facing upwards, overlapping one facing downwards. Actually, it's more interlocking crystalline tetrahedrons, triangular pyramids facing up and down. This structure can be used for traveling to subtle realms once it's activated. I think of the heart as being the center of this structure – the access point, where Heaven and Earth meet or join together, where physicality meets the spiritual realms. In my morning meditation sessions, I often see the top of the Merkabah, and hear (or say) the activation code which allows me to rise upwards. After some time enjoying the bliss of the space above the crown chakra (we'll get to that soon), I always return my energy to the heart. Here is where the communication with Guidance is received, the *Anahata* chakra.

The nature of our inner selves is bliss. Bringing that upper-level energy into the heart allows that bliss to manifest as devotion, gratitude, compassion, a thankfulness for All. We can label it by so many names, but it's an energy, an openness to receive, a receptive state of being that brings these benevolent forces into consciousness. It fills the heart to overflowing – a state of grace. When I did the first channeled self-portrait, which I describe in *Soul Map*, I was told to expand the "halo" which I often painted around the heads of my flying figures, to include the heart. The heart chakra needs to be included in any access to higher consciousness.

My guru, Muktananda, offered two basic teachings: *God dwells within you as you*, and *See God in each other.* Substitute the label The All or the Universe or Higher Consciousness for this if you want to – what you call that higher-level energy is up to you. I just want to get past the label(s) to explain these two concepts. With meditation practice comes the awareness of this higher consciousness – we tap into something greater than ourselves. We come to identify with That, or Self, rather than the contracted ego, or self. I understand that I am an expression of the Divine. It then follows that I can't help but honor myself, bow to myself, and develop myself to the most expanded version of myself as possible. I think highly of my Self – not because of any ego, but because I am That.

At the same time, if I am an expression of the Divine, you must be too – hence the second half of the teaching to see God in each other. When we say, *namaste*, which has become a common term in western culture these days, we are in fact honoring the sacred or divine that exists in another person. When we meditate and tap into the higher Self, and especially the Heart, our hearts fill with compassion – the understanding that we are each a part of The All, each a part of the Divine. Now we want the best for others, we think highly of others, we want others to be able to develop the greatest expression of who they are, because they're us. We're not separate, we form an interconnected whole. In our new time on Earth, in our ascended or elevated version of Earth, we will be more heart centered. We are becoming more heart centered. We hear others' stories, and we *feel* something. We feel the compassion within the heart. Perhaps more than anything, this is why opening the heart is so essential right now. Not only do we want to communicate with the upper realms, but we want to create a new Earth which includes All of us, the fullest expression of Who We Are.

Let's revisit our chakra journey so far. We began connecting with the Earth and the root chakra, giving us a stable foundation of security and balance. From there we rose to the sacral chakra, where we found our ability to create, to bring forth the lives we want to live. Rising to the solar plexus gave us a connection to our emotions, our clear intention and sense of personal power. And now we step into the heart, our soul's seat, our appreciation and gratitude, our deep connection with others and The All. Each chakra is built upon the next and cannot exist alone. Each depends on the efficiency of the others, so that all together they operate or co-operate for the purpose of manifesting a full expression of who we are at the deepest level of being.

Often there's much healing to do in the heart because of the injuries we've suffered in this life, and also what we've brought with us from past lives to work on in this one. Disappointments, losses, traumas all leave scarring, which impact our relationship with ourselves and with others – especially others we hold dear. Healing these injuries, as painful as that may be, is necessary. Our hearts are key to creating a new Earth. We cannot drag the old stuff with us – we've got to find a way of release, soothing the hurts, and filling the heart with love. I'm not talking about the romantic love depicted by Hollywood, which comes and goes, dependent on attachment. This is an opening of the energetic heart, to feel appreciation of what we have, gratitude for the wonder of it All, caring and compassion for both us and for others. These are the expressions of the heart with which we wish to color new Earth, where all beings are honored and cherished.

How do we do that? How do we heal the heart? Personally, I think meditation is key. Meditation gives us the ability to go within, to contemplate the heart, to open it, to make the connection with Guides who are around to help us heal. The heart is a portal, a way in, a means of connecting on the deepest level to the Cosmos. It's also a station to receive communications. Guides will tell us what's necessary for healing. In our culture, we tend to think we have to do this on our own. Practitioners can help, but the inner work can be guided by Ascended Masters, Archangels, and angelic guides, as well as spirit guides (people who have passed over). When I do the guided visualization where we welcome our "guide" into our heart chamber, it's always Sananda who appears to me (the soul level of Jesus). Keep in mind, I was raised as a nice, Jewish girl, so this was initially a bit difficult for me to reconcile. However, I realized (aside from the fact that he was a Jewish rabbi) that the connection I have with him transcends the dogmatic confines of religion, and that I have worked with him for many, probably uncountable, lifetimes. And although I also communicate with angelic guides who speak to me during meditation focused within the heart, they are associated with Archangel Michael. And sometimes direct communication takes place from Archangel Metatron. But it's always Sananda who appears during that particular visualization, always dressed in white robes, appearing much like the paintings we know of Jesus. The heart is a happening place when it's open.

Expressive arts can also help in the healing process, the process of letting go of past hurts, and opening to what's possible. Simply by focusing on the heart while using any of the modalities, we gain access. But meditation or visualization beforehand will unlock the door, just as George Harrison sang in *Behind that Locked Door*.

> Why are you still crying?
> Your pain is now through
> Please forget those teardrops
> Let me take them for you
> The love you are blessed with
> This world's waiting for
> So let out your heart please, please
> From behind that locked door.

George Harrison

These songs came through George Harrison to awaken us, to guide us, to show us the way.

Meditation on the Heart

Meditating from or on the heart chakra can be powerful. What I've discovered through my own practice is that it's not a matter of imagining or visualizing what *can* happen in the heart, but noticing what *is* happening in the heart. As I focus on the heart center, I feel a fullness. As I continue, I notice a complete stillness. Everything comes to rest. I could sit there all day. Words fall away, thoughts fall away. I am simply sitting in that energy. Now at the same time, I am in a receptive state, and so if there is a message to come through from Guidance (whatever the source), I will hear that. If I want to remember it, I must write it down as soon as I stop my meditation, or else it is gone, much like writing down a dream after it happens. Unless it has a profound impact, a dream will dissipate quickly because the dream state is an altered state of consciousness. So is meditation. For me, sometimes the messages are simple sentences; other times, they are longer channelings, which require recording on some level – either writing or audio recording. I was told early in my learning process that it is important to write the messages down. Not only is it a way to remember the information, but it's also a validation that it's actually happened. You aren't imagining it!

Heart Meditation

Go ahead, enter your meditative state through whatever process works best for you. Focusing on the point or space between the inbreath and the outbreath is a gateway into the Self. Once you have entered that inner space, focus on the heart. Take your time. What do you notice? How does it feel? Simply sit in that inner energy.

If you want, try listening for guidance…it's subtle at first. Trust it. Or if you prefer, just sit in the stillness of the heart.

White Light Meditation/ Visualization in the Heart Chamber

In the *Higher Chakras* chapter, I've included a full white light meditation that you can use as a guided meditation. Either record it for yourself, speaking *very slowly* and pausing where it's noted – the slower the better, or have someone read it *s l o w l y* for you. When you are on the return trip up through the chakra system, there is a visualization within the heart chamber. Here is that visualization, but remember, it's taken out of context. One of the reasons this visualization works is that you've already been absorbed in a deep meditation experience, so that guidance is readily accessible. I suggest doing the whole process if you can. My experience leading others through this brief process is how surprisingly accessible guidance can be. Our guides are always with us; we just need to be open to acknowledging their presence.

Visualization in the Heart Chamber

After entering your state of meditation, focus on the heart and imagine an emerald, green glow. Take some time with this:

Imagine that within the heart, there is a room – a chamber. You can decorate your heart chamber anyway you wish (pause)... *There is a seat for your soul to sit upon, and you sit down upon the seat... There's a knock at the door and you rise to answer it. You open the door, and there standing in the doorway is your guide. What do they look like? How are they dressed? Who is it? Perhaps they will tell you their name... Invite your guide into your heart chamber, to sit next to you on your seat. If you have a question that you'd like to ask your guide, go ahead and do it now, and receive the answer... Open your eyes slowly, wiggle your hands and feet.*

Write down what you received. Be sure to include who your guide was, how they appeared, and what they said.

WAVE from the Heart #1

Materials: paint, ½" – 1" paintbrush(es), palette, water container, large paper, notebook

- Set up for painting (see supply list)

- **Meditation:** Begin with a meditation on the heart.

- **Painting:** play a heart-centered instrumental
  Continue the energy you experienced in meditation with painting. (Be sure to add enough water to your acrylics so they really flow). As always, don't worry about form, just paint the energy – whatever comes through for you.

- **Movement:** Using the same music, contemplate your painting, then move to it. Feel the movement from the inside out – just let yourself go.

- **Free writing:** write whatever comes to mind.

WAVE from the Heart #2

Materials: your choice

- **Meditation:** if meditating in a group, sit in a circle. Consciously connect with other members of the group by sending a ray of light from your heart to others' hearts before you begin.
  Go ahead and meditate, shifting your energy to the heart. Contemplate the energy within the heart. What do you notice? Stay there until you're having a deep experience of heart energy. You can do this with or without meditative music (I prefer without).

- **Toning:** Without music, keeping the eyes closed, allow the sounds to come – only vowels, you can play with the sounds, high or low, letting the notes choose you. If you're in a group, keep one ear open to the sound of the group. The toning will come to a natural end on its own.

- **Choice of expression:** ground the energy by doing a modality of your choice: it could be free writing, poetry, painting, movement, or whatever calls to you in the moment.

- **Offering to the group:** if you're working in a group, form a standing circle. Each person offers a gesture with a sound to the group. The group repeats it.

WAVE from the Heart #3

Materials: your choice, notebook

As described in chapter one, we are energetic beings; we exude energy, creating our energy field. That is what people experience when they come physically near us, whether they're aware of it or not. And those of us who are particularly empathic will sense or read the energy – it impacts us. When we're in a crowded room, there's a lot of energy, because everyone's energy is being emitted into the collective space. This is why public spaces can be challenging to an empath – we feel and absorb all that energy. I usually can't sleep well after teaching a class of thirty students in a contained classroom because I've taken all that energy into my system. Students are releasing their stress, their anxiety, their suppressed emotion through their work. Where does that energy go? Into the room. Into the environment. Those sensitives among us will sense it.

As we do the exploratory work, we reach a point in our process where these energies are being transmuted – turned into something else. So, they are not just being released, but changed into something more beneficial – perhaps more peaceful, perhaps more exuberant...whatever that is, we start to develop a sense of well-being. And *that* energy is emanating from our energy fields. For example, after a deep, guided meditation, students *feel* the change in the atmosphere. There is a strong sense of peace and wellbeing.

Meditation on the heart is an opportunity to do some alchemy – to change that energy. If we are overly anxious, struggling to find a sense of safety from the root connection to the Earth, or emotionally overwrought, overworking our solar plexus, we come into the meditation distraught. Meditation in general, but more specifically from the heart, can transform or transmute that into peacefulness. Part of greater self-awareness is being conscious of the energy we are putting out into the world, into our shared energy field, the sum total of all of our collective frequencies. A mandala, as discussed in the modalities section of the book, allows us to make that heart energy visible.

- Meditation on the heart
- Draw or paint within a traced circle, as large as possible. Choose your medium of preference.
- Write a poem (form doesn't matter, it doesn't need to rhyme, it's simply a free flow of energy using words).

Channeling: *Opened, Attuned, Aligned...*

Here, within the heart, we speak to you, for it is from this center where the portal opens to the multidimensions within your very being. You have these entry points which can take you beyond this world, and in fact beyond your solar system and galaxy to a broader, more expanded...consciousness. This transmission is in that way slower...because of the distance it travels to your receptors. And it is from this place within the heart that this transmission is received... (you are chosen in this way to communicate this material*) to others who may come upon this book, this written form of relayed information. You were visited this morning by one of our favorites, yes - it is an intimate relationship of yours from eons past. It was good to be reunited – there was much symbolism within that dream, that visitation, yes, which you recognized, for the new heart knows its deepest connections are perceived and recognized. Your guidance comes to you in many forms relayed from multidimensions. Your ability to travel upwards using your Merkabah light body system, operating system, enables you to receive this information through your heart chakra. And so we would say to anyone who wishes to receive such communication *to develop their abilities to travel within that light body, the very center of which is this heart, yes, heart...where the portals are accessed... (Opened, attuned, aligned, you have that perception which allows you to hear, to see, to know all....This is all we wish to communicate to you in this time, at this moment, we sing to you, for you have received guidance from the musical realm of this guide. Guru Om, and many, many blessings to you*). Go in peace.*

*What is in parentheses was sung. Actually, many words in this channeling were sung. I did, in fact, have an extended and very vivid "dream" – more like a visitation, with George Harrison just before I woke on this particular morning. I thought it also significant that George came through again, weeks after I'd written the above text about the heart chakra when he'd brought through the lyrics of *Behind That Locked Door*. In this morning dream, George was wearing a crocheted elephant tie or scarf, the trunk of which I kissed – Ganesha, the Hindu elephant deity, clears the path of obstacles for us to create new beginnings. It goes without saying, I appreciated this sign of support, as well as George's sense of humor.

Lord Ganesha, Remover of Obstacles

Chapter 7
Open the Throat and Sing

I'm writing this in the order of the chakras from bottom (Root) to top (Soul Star). It's hard to move on from the heart, but we don't leave the heart behind. We are continuing to build our energetic system as we rise higher toward the heavens. The throat, or *Vishuddha,* is colored a rich cobalt blue. It represents our self-expression, speaking our truth, and generally being heard. The throat chakra energy allows us to put ourselves out in the world.

I find working with women, that we often have a challenge with the throat. We have been taught as girls to be silent, allowing others to speak, not drawing attention to our (true) selves. I believe centuries of silencing and persecution when we have spoken our truth (i.e., the martyrs throughout the ages), have created well-ingrained patterns of inner and outer silencing. I have past life memories of neck-related death because of speaking out, which have manifested in this life as fear to speak (I had a phone phobia in my early twenties). I ran small groups of women's personal growth groups for years, which felt comfortable, until I finally began teaching at the college level, when I was forced to speak in front of large groups of students. If, as I believe, we come into this life to work through our personal issues, including those of past life trauma, then this was the perfect opportunity for me to do that work. It took years to overcome my reticence to speak, though I did find my sense of humor was a helpful tool – teaching became a form of performance art. As I did more spiritual work and became practiced in teaching, which included speaking my truth, my authentic self emerged. My fear of speaking dissipated. In other words, just as we must engage in creativity to become more creative, I needed to speak in order to develop my voice. Expressive arts strengthen voice, and I'm not talking only about our physical voice here. I mean developing self-confidence to put ourselves out there. We must speak in order to be heard, whether that means talking or showing our art or performing - presenting our most authentic selves. It may require courage, but without exercising self-expression, we will remain stifled and unfulfilled. In order to become the fullest expression of who we are, and to add that to the Collective Pie of which we are an essential part, we must reclaim our ability to express ourselves as fully as we can. We must open our throats and sing. The world needs us now more than ever.

WAVE #1: Opening the Throat

Materials: paint, large paper

- **Meditation on the Throat**

    As you enter your meditative state, bring your attention to the throat area. Imagine the throat filled with a brilliant, cobalt blue light. See the throat chakra opening, and filling with more and more of this brilliant blue light. Imagine yourself sounding – perhaps you're at the top of a hill, somewhere that your voice will carry a long distance. Imagine yourself opening the throat and sounding, fully and clearly. Do any issues come up for you? Is there something holding you back from doing this? What is that? Let the answer come to you…

    Try it again, just imagining the sound. What would happen if you felt joy as you sounded? What if you felt free? Simply contemplate this, as you focus on the throat.

- **Creative Movement and Sound**

    Choose free-flowing instrumental music to play. Go ahead, move to the music. Feel the music entering every limb, using the entire space to move your body. Move your *whole* body. Now, as you move around your space, feeling the energy from the inside out (don't worry about form, only tapping the energy of the music), begin to sound. Just play with the sound. See how your movements connect with the sound. How can you allow your body to move with the sound?

    In a group: Do the first part of the movement and sound individually, then find a partner. Continue with the sound and movement, but one person leads and the other mimics their actions. Don't forget the sound!! Then, join with another pair, and continue doing this as a group of 4. Allow free movement, experiencing it as a form of play.

- **Painting with Sound**

    Working individually, use paints as you respond to the music. Make sounds as you paint. See if you can make sweeping motions, using the entire paper.

- **Sound and movement**

    Individually or in a group: make a sound and movement to express your current feeling(s).

WAVE #2: Speaking your Truth

Materials: roll of paper, paints and/or oil pastels

I once met a lawyer who attended a No Limits for Women Artists workshop. At first, I didn't understand why she was in the group – she wasn't an artist. But she explained that thinking of her work in court as performance art allowed her to speak more authentically. Preparing her presentation was a stressful, cerebral exercise for her, filled with concerns for what she *should* say. But perceiving her courtroom "performance" as art, as full expression from the inside out, came from her truth, allowing the words to flow. Opening the throat means allowing your voice to sound from its authentic source.

The advantage of attentive listening is that it's a process of thinking out loud. We don't need to know what we're going to say ahead of time. The more we participate in it, the more able we are to trust our voice. Just like scribbling or any of the other modalities, it doesn't need to be perfect. It's not the form that matters; it's the message or thought that counts. And with practice, that will begin to flow. Remember these guidelines for attentive listening:

Confidentiality is crucial for feeling safe to open up to another.

Listener: Try not to think about what you will say when it's your turn; otherwise, you're not really listening. Do not interrupt the speaker. This is not a conversation.

Fill your entire time – keep talking until the timer indicates the end of your time. You may find you go deeper this way.

Remember, it's a process of thinking out loud – you don't need to know what you're going to say.

Don't comment on what someone has said without their permission; we are not here to give advice. We fully trust that the speaker has the inner wisdom to figure things out themselves. We are only holding *safe* space for them to do their work.

- **Writing** (individually) or **Attentive Listening** (with a partner or in a small group)

   If I were to choose one thing that matters most to me, what would that be? (Don't overthink this – we'll be doing more with this in the chapter on the Crown chakra and spirit.) Write as much as you want, or if doing attentive listening, set the timer for each participant for 2 or 3 minutes.

- **Drawing** or **painting:** Hang large paper on the wall if possible; otherwise, simply use your large drawing paper on your usual flat surface. Use your medium of choice. If you're doing this in a group, give each other turns to do this.

   Make a broad stroke or shape on the paper, and then make a confident statement afterwards. If doesn't matter what you say, only that you say it! Some examples might be: *This is a circle! I painted blue! I am strong! I'm free! I love this!* It doesn't matter, what you say, only that it's true in the moment. There is a certain amount of improvisation in this, so just wing it. Don't think. Let the truth be expressed (or express the truth).

   A variation would be to make the statement AS you are drawing/painting. Or to make sound as you are drawing/painting.

- **Sound and movement**

   Make an authentic sound and movement for how you're feeling. If in a group, each take a turn, respecting each person's expression.

WAVE #3

Materials: notebook, oil pastels or paint, large paper

- **Wild writing**

  Choose a topic, any topic. Set the timer for 10 minutes and start to write. Remember, don't pay any attention to form, grammar, or spelling. If you change direction, go with it...just keep it going. Don't think, don't pause... Just let it rip!

- **Scribbling with oil pastels or paint**

  Put on some lively energetic music and continue the energy of the wild writing – in the same way, call it *wild scribbling!* with absolutely NO thought about form, line, or color (though you can change colors at any time), LET IT RIP!! Fill the page!

- **Movement:**

  Individually: look at your drawing/painting. Contemplate it. Move to it. Then, write a statement: I am _____. Write as much as you want.

  In a group: Form a circle.

  - Locking arms, move forward making sound (don't decide ahead of time, just improvise), and then back again. Repeat.

  - Unlock your arms. Step back a little, keeping your place in the circle. Do a little dance which expresses your experience with the scribbling. This can be done simultaneously, everyone at once. Or, in a well-established group, you can take turns.

  - Taking turns, make a statement: I am _____.

Channeling the Ones: The Divine Feminine Power

*Greetings. We understand you wish us to speak on the topic of the throat chakra for here is a place within the body where one's essence is allowed to reach others through this expression, through…the operation of this energy center. This center can be shut down easily from the trauma of past experience, whether that be in this lifetime or another. The soul is imprinted by trauma. Many women on Earth have a history of systemic trauma for having spoken their truth and suffered from the persecution resulting from that. And so there is much to heal here, not just on an individual level, but for the greater collective energy, for it is now at this particular time, you see, that the Divine Feminine energy is rising on your planet and this center of the throat must be opened to its fullest extent. This requires the healing of that past trauma. We find then the exercising of this chakra when women amass to protest the limitations imposed upon them by those in authority. Women do not wish to be oppressed by such authority and wish to have autonomy within themselves. **Now** is the time for **that power** to come to the forefront. **Now** is the time for the Divine Feminine to balance the powers upon the planet. This means that women must unleash their inner fire, their inner flame, and allow it to be seen and heard to its fullest. This also means for the men upon the planet to seek within themselves their gentleness, their nurturing, feminine presence for this planet requires delicacy. This planet requires a nurturing energy, for it needs to restore itself to its true balance. So you see, the throat chakra has much to do with this coming to power of the Divine Feminine energy at this time. Women must sing. Women must shout. Women must unleash that primal power within for the nurturance of all. Nurturance has a strength. Nurturance is all-encompassing. It is more than just a gentle hug. It is the birthing of the new planet, of a new way of being. This is true power. And so, we would say to you to have a most exquisite day and enjoy yourselves in this time of life here and now.*

Chapter 8
Pure Vision: The Third Eye

Om Tat Sat

As I complete the throat chakra section and prepare to begin this next chapter on the Third Eye, I hear *Om Tat Sat*: The Supreme Truth or Supreme Reality. Ultimately, our goal is to experience That. I am reminded that my Guides have advised me to "Go within, attune, and align." As I tune into these energy centers in the *shushuma*, they align into one integrated system, leading from our Earth connection to the heavens above. Open alignment offers that experience of Oneness, of Truth, of our Divine Nature if you will. As I attune to the third eye, automatically the chakras below – throat and heart, along with those underlying these, contribute their support, connection, or frequency. I do not experience these chakras in isolation – they are interconnected. What is the Source of Om Tat Sat? It's not the throat, it's not the third eye, it's that totality.

After learning to meditate by focusing on the third eye (between the eyebrows), and synchronizing my breath with a mantra suggested to me by my guru, Swami Muktananda, who also granted me *shaktipat*, or the awakening of the *kundalini* which lies dormant at the base of the spine, I've come to expect to see what he called 'the blue pearl' – a sesame seed sized blue light in my third eye. In Baba's book, *Play of Consciousness*, he described a series of openings, which happened during the unfolding of his developing and deepening meditation process - the appearance of inner lights which mark the different levels or aspects of the body, "the four levels of the individual soul": first the red of the physical body - the full size of the body; then the white flame of the subtle body, the size of the thumb; then the black of the causal body, the size of a fingertip; and finally the blue pearl of the supra-causal body, the size of a sesame seed.[10] The blue pearl is ephemeral, lasting only a second, but I also find that when I've been meditating deeply and regularly, I see patches of this blue light when I close my eyes. Although the *bindi* that devotees wear on their foreheads in the location of the third eye is red, the actual color of *Shakti* is this brilliant blue. Baba defines *Shakti* as "divine conscious energy" or the Divine Feminine Principle. He wrote: "When the latent treasure of inner Shakti is released in meditation, you will soon ascend to higher meditative stages. You will see splendid sights and glorious forms. You will apprehend internal divine lights."

The third eye chakra, or *Ajna*, is not surprisingly related to inner vision – being able to perceive where we are going – seeing what's up ahead. It enhances clairvoyance, being able to imagine and envision what we are creating. I think I've always had a developed third eye – it helped me in school because my memory was visual. I could SEE what I was supposed to remember. I do believe that artists have a strong spatial intelligence, which psychologist Howard Gardner noted in his revolutionary work on multiple intelligences.[11] It may also enhance one's ability to focus on the third eye in meditation. Being able to see what's coming up, being able to call upon this strength, has allowed me to see my path ahead. Combined

---

[10] Swami Muktananda Paramahansa, *Play of Consciousness*. California, Shree Gurudev Siddha Yoga Ashram, 1974.
[11] Howard Gardner, *Frames of Mind*. Portsmouth, Heinemann, 1984.

with the intuition I experience from my solar plexus (gut), this gives me the capability to make plans and move in a particular direction with a sense of assuredness.

I certainly could not have channeled the energy mandalas that my Guides (particularly Metatron) relayed to me without seeing them in great detail, in full color. And although you will often hear (including in this text) to meditate through the heart, in my opinion, it begins with the third eye, increasing your ability to focus, to imagine, to see. An opened third eye is a wonderful thing.

WAVE #1: Developing Vision

Materials: paints, large paper, notebook

- **Meditation on the Third Eye**
  Breathe, letting go of all tension. Begin to focus on the breath, and more specifically, on the point where the inbreath meets the outbreath, and vice versa. If your attention wanders, bring your attention back to the breath. Keep your closed eyes focused on the space between the eyebrows. As your meditation deepens, what do you notice?

- **Painting**
  Using meditative music (search third eye), simply paint the energy you are feeling, sensing, or what you saw or observed during the meditation. Again – it doesn't need to have form; it's the energy we're interested in here.

- **Free writing**

WAVE #2

Materials: magazines, scissors, glue stick, paper or cardstock

- **Visualization: where are you going?**

    Close your eyes, tune into the breath. After a few moments, contemplate your life as it is right now (pause)… Now imagine yourself 5 years from now…how do you look? What are you doing? (pause) 10 years from now… how do you look? What are you doing? (pause). When you're ready, open your eyes.

- **Collage:**

    As you contemplate your future self, look through magazines for words, images, and colors that present themselves to you (not looking for specifics). What words, images, and colors call to you? Cut as many as you can, then assemble them in any way you choose.

- **Writing:**

    What do you know about yourself now? Write as much as you want.

Visioning without Resistance

It's important to be able to imagine what you want for yourself in your life and to verbalize it. Saying it out loud lends power to it, allowing you to take yourself seriously. Saying it with witnesses provides the opportunity for commitment and follow-through: now it's not just my desire, but someone has heard me say it; I guess I'd better make it happen. The issue with creating a vision for yourself of what you want in your life, is that it can seem intimidating, but by breaking it down to what your next step is, all you have to accomplish is this one thing (until the next session). Since we've all internalized certain messages from society's value system, which limit our self-confidence and commitment to our own process, it's important to identify the beliefs we're holding about ourselves and contradict them, so they no longer hold power over us. Finally, by pulling in unconditional support, we surround ourselves with those who want to see us succeed. I learned these steps through artist Betsy Damon's No Limits for Women Artists, which was a format for women artists (all women, really) to realize their largest visions for themselves. The work is most effective being done in a regular group, but you can also do it individually through writing, as long as you have the required support. Here are the 4 basic questions:

- **What's my largest vision for myself?** Go as big as you want. Get extravagant. Get detailed. Or keep it simple – it's up to you. In a group, say it out loud. Time each person's turn, so that everyone gets equal time. In No Limits, we did all 4 questions in 8 minutes, or you can break them down to a certain number of minutes per question, each participant in turn answering the first question, then the second, and so on.

- **What's my next step?** This needs to be something doable – it might be making a phone call, or contacting something who has information for you; it might be doing some research or finishing a project… Each time you meet with your group (we met regularly, every 2 or 3 weeks), chances are you will have done that step and will be ready for next. Inevitably, you end up at your initial vision (or some version of it).

- **Where does it get difficult?** After stating what's been hard for you, you can ask, what must I believe that I'm having this problem continuing with my vision/my work/my life? The No Limits leader might ask you to state the opposite. For example, if a woman felt she didn't have the financial resources to buy her art supplies, you might be asked to say, *my art has value;* or *the world needs my art*. There's an emotional charge attached to the statement, so making sound like *UHN!* or a physical movement like stamping your foot, or simply stating it with conviction: *my art has value in the world!!!* helps to cut through your attachment or dependence on the limiting belief. You don't have to rely on a leader, however, to do this work. You can do it yourself. I believe that every person has the innate capacity to work through their issues, with support. Every person, given safe space, will move toward self-discovery and self-knowledge. It's the commitment to your personal process and the unconditional support of others which will keep you moving.

- **Where do you or will you find support?** Who are the people you can rely on? Who are the people who won't judge you, that you can trust to be there for you? Personally, I've found I have close women friends who provide this for me, as I in turn provide it to them. But I also have my angelic and spirit guides who support me. Not all support is the kind that can be seen.

Adding Expressive Arts to the Visioning Process

I found that doing the visioning work was very effective for my group members. Women stayed in the group for long stretches of time, committed to their development, and willing to show up to do the work. But I noticed that after I added expressive arts to the mix, it was easier/gentler to work through the third question of what is difficult or blocking one's process. As participants worked with the various modalities, they became aware of their own impediments, and by making sense of it through free writing or to others in explaining their work, they knew what they had to do. They automatically stated their contradictions to what was limiting them (sounding much like affirmations). Expressive arts also aid us in working through that emotional charge as we let go of the limiting beliefs, often released in the forms of sound and movement.

WAVE #3

Materials: oil or chalk pastels, large paper, notebook

- **The 4 questions** (either out loud in a group or individually through writing):
    - What's my largest vision for myself? Or what do I want to create in my life?
    - What's my next step?
    - Where does it get difficult, or where do I get stuck?
    - Where will I find, or do I find support?

- **Where does it get difficult?** oil or chalk pastel scribbling/drawing.

    Close your eyes and focus on what you said when you answered the third question: where does it get difficult? Put on some instrumental music, and scribble or draw it out: Be aware of thoughts and feelings. Again, you don't need to know what it will be or how it will look. You'll know when you're done. If working in a group, be sure to give each person time to finish.

- **Writing Choices:**

- - Free writing
  - State your contradiction (affirmation) and write about it.

- **Share your drawing and process**, and then state your contradiction (with conviction).

- **Sound and Movement:** in a group, each take a turn to make an authentic sound and movement.

Channeling the Ones

Yes, we are with you at this time, wishing to speak upon the subject of what you would call the Third Eye, the inner vision, the ability to see what lies ahead for you in your future or perhaps as it is for you now. For vision takes on a deeper level of perception from this inner energetic state of being, more so than if you were to even contemplate your life from a waking state, for from this perspective, from this deeper level of perception, you can see and detect more. And so, we would say, at this time of evolution, during this extraordinary time of change, we find that many depend upon the old paradigm, the old third-dimensional way of seeing their lives, seeing their world, rather than exploring what is possible. For you see, the old is disappearing and along with it, the old ways of doing things, the old ways of creation are also disappearing. It is up to you at this time to re-imagine what it is you wish to prefer and to see your lives, not as singular areas of activity, but to see them integrated and synthesized with each other, so that perhaps you would have in the past pursued one area of your creativity, whereas now you are pursuing many and they do not stand alone, but they are supported by each other, you see. It becomes one fuller expression of who you are as an energetic being, connected not only to Earth, but to all realms of energy, all realms of activity, all realms of being. And there are many ways of being beyond the physical. And so, you see that there is a new...ah...we hesitate to use the word paradigm, for it is in a sense a way of organizing the Universe, whereas we are in the process of re-organizing the Universe according to newer or new principles. And so, let us call it a web, perhaps a network of new energetic interconnections which you are, as you are re-imagining, creating. Therefore, we would say, not to think of the individual or singular activity in isolation, but to see your entirety, your wholeness, evolve into one multidimensional expression, and in that sense, in your receptivity, which is in a sense an active way of perceiving, to see that, to perceive the possibility of that expression appearing in the world. And that is a new form of manifestation. So, as you move forward, you may think of your lives as synthesized and coming forth into the new world as this multilayered, multidimensional expression of who you are now, and who you are becoming. And so, we would say to you to go in peace and to enjoy your day.

Vision   Nancy Winternight

Chapter 9
The Crown Chakra: Spirit and My Connection to All That Is

And so, we move higher. Of all the chakras, perhaps the Crown is my favorite. It is the place I most frequently hang out during meditation. The Crown, or *Sahasrara*, is the location of spirit – who we are in this lifetime, with all that encompasses, most especially what we are here to do. Yes, we each have a purpose to fulfill; we have dropped into the families we have in order to work through the karmic conditions which will allow us to fulfill that purpose and become the fullest expression of who we are. Sometimes there's much healing to do to attain that – growth is a life-long task, and a life-long attainment.

When I meditate and focus on the Crown – a simple raising of my awareness one step above the third eye, I pass through a gateway into higher level energy. I can feel as if I'm levitating, because of its connection with All That Is. In other words, I can focus my attention on the Crown and experience its particular energy, but because it's a gateway, I can rise even higher to experience upper realms…that's coming in my discussion of the Soul Star and beyond. The Crown is the access point.

Unsurprisingly (to me), the color associated with the Crown chakra is purple or violet. My favorite color? Purple. Show me anything purple – I must immediately have it. I have purple frames for my glasses, purple shoes, purple purse, purple clothing…I immerse myself in it as if I cannot get enough of it. It's where my spirit resides.

One of the issues people experience is not knowing what their purpose is; they wander from one job to another, never really finding what they're supposed to do with their lives. I see students in this predicament. Forced to declare their major, they have to decide which path to take, when they can't see the path that they want or any path at all. I think our educational system does a disservice by providing a cookie cutter education – everyone learning the same subject matter in the same way at the same time, all very prescribed with sameness – how to do it, when to do it, even why to do it. Some of my first jobs as a professor are to foster creativity, a return to their innate sensibility, and supporting them to reclaim their autonomy and become aware of their preferences, their desires, their *excitement*, which is key to knowing yourself and your purpose. What excites you? That's what you need to be doing. It's your nervous system directing you in the right direction.

If our educational system were less uniform, less based in conformity, students could explore their interests. *Neti, neti*, from Hindu scripture - *not this, not this*, describes the process of eliminating what is NOT our truth, till we eventually land there. Exploration, experimentation, permission to fail, are all essential pieces to the process of knowing oneself. We are drawn to certain activities because they resonate with us. Our development must include the time and space to discover that – or at a higher level, That. I am That That I am. Aligning with the Self is key, and the Crown chakra can take you there, to that inner place where spirit resides.

During my preparation to channel the *Sacred Geometry* energy mandala series, I was shown in meditation Da Vinci's *Vitruvian Man*. If you saw it, you'd recognize it – legs together and apart, arms outstretched to the side and raised, within a circle and a square. I was also urged to do some research on the Kabbalah Tree of Life, which up until that point I had a desire to explore but was unfamiliar with. I had also begun to automatically perform something with my hands at the point during meditation where I shifted my attention from the crown chakra to the heart. In fact, I still do this: I raise my hands up and make a sweeping motion as if tracing a hood from above the Crown to my shoulders, three times. And then I move my hand from the top of my head down to my heart. I did not know why I did this, only that I did and continue to do so, and that it helps me to transition my attention from upper chakras to the heart. Looking at the Tree of Life diagram, I understand these energetic movements. [12]

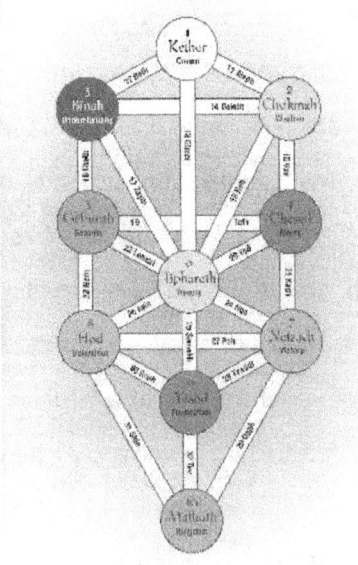

---

[12] Tim Dedopulos, *Kabbalah: An illustrated introduction to the esoteric heart of Jewish mysticism*. New York, Gramercy Books, 2005.

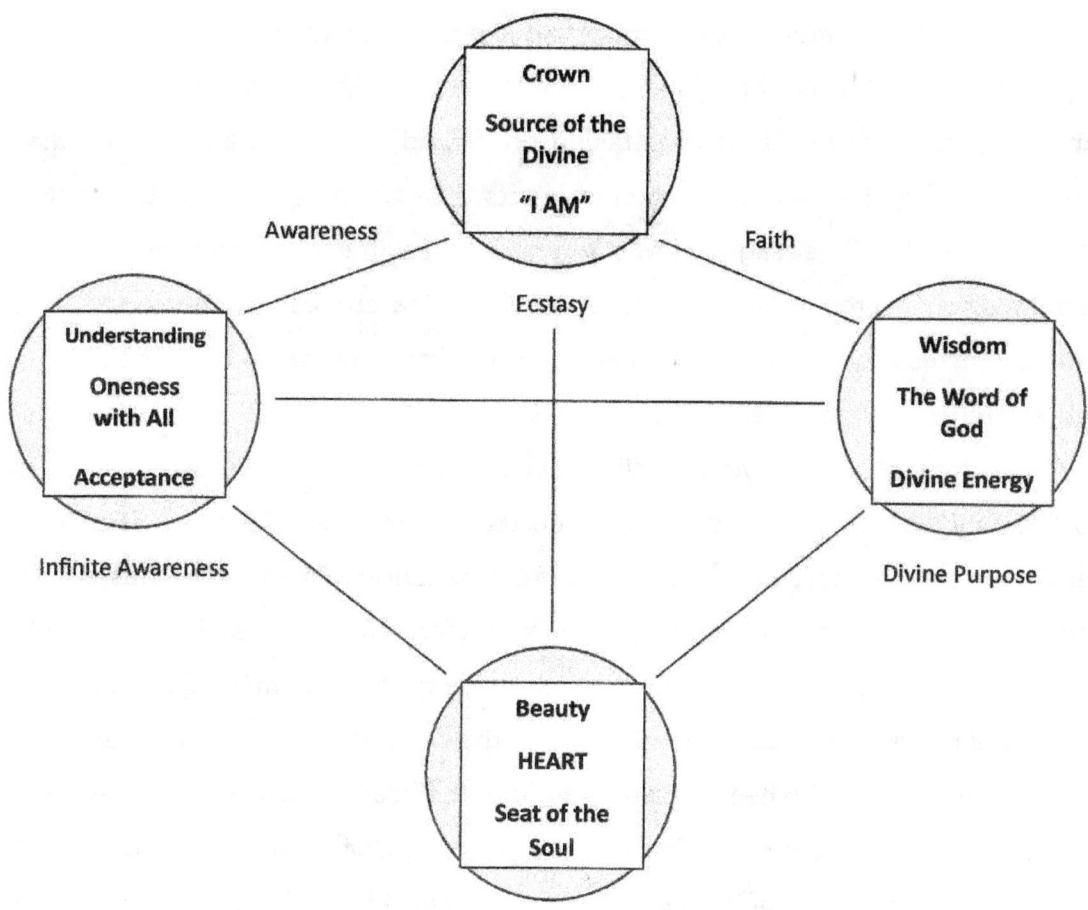

Tree of Life

Here is the upper section of the Kabbalah Tree of Life. Note the Crown at the top.
The heart is located at the center of the Tree.

At the very top of the Tree of Life is the Crown, the Source of the Divine, the *I Am*. No duality exists here – it is One, and its nature is ecstasy (I use the word bliss). Mm hmm. I realized at once that this is where I hang out in meditation, at the Crown. Who doesn't want to experience ecstasy? Isn't that what taking drugs and sex are all about? Isn't that what everyone's chasing? But here it is, no side effects. Just Oneness with the Divine. Now...in the diagram, you'll see that slightly lower to the right is witness consciousness, the location of wisdom, divine energy, ecstatic meditation, AND divine purpose, connected to the Crown by faith. By increasing our faith, we come to know that purpose. On the left side, we see infinite awareness, or spiritual awareness, a sense of Oneness with All – Understanding. There's no sense of the individual self or ego, and time does not exist. There is total acceptance and reception. This state is connected to the Crown by awareness. These are powerful concepts, or more accurately, powerful experiences. The motion I was/am doing in my meditation is in fact connecting the Crown with these two aspects: the wisdom of divine energy/purpose and spiritual awareness/understanding. Then, by moving my hand from the Crown to the Heart (in the diagram we see it is the Seat of the Soul), I am connecting the Divine and the Soul. Then, when I meditate through the heart, which we are called to do now to raise our frequency, I am anchoring the energy of the Divine within the Seat of the Soul. I can then receive the divine guidance within the heart chakra. As I said, these energy centers of the body do not exist in isolation. This is a system, designed to work in synthesis, all parts together – one operating system. In fact, we can look at the Tree of Life diagram and relate it to the chakra system – all the parts are there.

    To me, the way to the Crown is through meditation. It requires a dedicated commitment to one's process of Becoming. It requires intention (will) and follow-through (action). It requires consistency. It also requires flexibility and humor – not everything will go your way; there will be interruptions and disruptions along the way. Recently, I was having a massage – a blissful massage I might add (I always enter a meditative state during massage with my skillful massage therapist – she says it's her 'calling'). The next-door neighbor started mowing their lawn right outside the window. Then the garbage truck stopped in front of the house…beep, beep, beep. Christine added time to the massage to compensate for these disruptions, but I told her I had heard the hum of the lawn mower reverberate in my root chakra – just an aspect of the meditation for me, and the garbage truck beeping resonated in my heart. To me, it was just sound…there is that total acceptance and reception from the Infinite Awareness aspect of the Tree of Life. I didn't mind having extra massage time, though. I had to laugh about it. In fact, I often laugh during meditation – perhaps it's that ecstasy. I always get up to meditate upon waking in the morning – why wouldn't I want that blissful, ecstatic experience?

The doorway to the Crown is through meditation. What I like to see, though, is what happens after that experience. I usually have students paint after meditation – fluidity of expression seems appropriate, though I myself have used chalk pastels to make mandalas after meditation. Movement is also good. I sometimes do creative movement right after meditation – it grounds the meditation energy, bringing it into the physicality of the body.

WAVE #1: Purpose

Materials: choice (collage or drawing with oil pastels), notebook

- **Attentive Listening (**with partner or small group) **or Journaling**

    - What excites you?
    - Are you doing that? If not, why not?
    - If you could create one thing in your life, what would it be?
    - What would you have to let go of to do that?

- **Sound and movement**

    Close your eyes, tune in, and make an authentic sound/movement from the inside out.

- **Choice:**

    - **Collage:** Search for words, images, and colors which stimulate or excite you.

    - **Drawing with oil pastels** (use some exciting instrumental music)

    As you think about what excites you, scribble on the paper with oil pastels. Let the excitement really come through your arm, your hand…be aware of thoughts and feelings. Then, **free write.**

WAVE #2: The Self

Materials: chalk pastels, large paper, notebook

- **Visualization:**

   Breathe, releasing all tension... As you tune inside, creating some inner space, begin to focus on the self... Who are you (pause)? What makes you uniquely you (pause)? What are the qualities that are your own (pause)? What is your energy (pause)?

- **Mandala of the Self,** with chalk pastels. Remember, we're making non-traditional mandalas (energy or artistic mandalas). I like to use sitar music for this, but you can use any music that resonates with the Crown chakra.

   Trace or draw a large circle on your paper. Let your energy flow onto the paper as you focus on who you are. Make a mandala of the self.

- **Writing prompt:** Begin your writing, *I am...*

   Take a break and continue...

WAVE #3: The World/Planet

Materials: chalk pastels, large paper, notebook

- **Visualization:**

   Breathe, releasing all tension... As you tune inside, creating some inner space, begin to focus on your relationship with the world... What do you have to offer the world (pause)? And what does the world have to offer you? What do you receive from the world (long pause)? Contemplate this exchange of energy, as you see yourself offering your energy to the world (long pause) …

Now see your relationship with the planet. Again, what do you have to offer the planet?... And what does the planet offer to you? What do you receive from the planet…? What do you wish for the planet…? Be sure to take plenty of time.

- **Mandala for the World or the Planet,** with chalk pastels. Again, we're making non-traditional mandalas (energy or artistic mandalas). Continue to use sitar music for this or use any music that resonates with the Crown chakra.

  After tracing or drawing a large circle on your paper, let your energy flow onto the paper as you focus on your relationship with either the world or the Earth, and what you have to offer it, or what you would wish for it. Make a mandala for the World or the Earth.

- **Writing prompt:** write a conversation between Self and World/Earth. What would they have to say to each other?

Going Deeper: Experiencing the Crown

Materials: chalk pastels or paint, large paper, notebook

- **Deep meditation**

  As you deepen your meditation, shift your attention from the third eye to the crown. Simply be there. What do you notice about the energy here? What do you notice about yourself? Sit for at least 10 minutes, 20 if you can.

- **Movement**

Using music that resonates with the Crown (HZ), move to the music. Honor the Earth and allow the energy to rise up into the body. Simply express yourself through the body. When you're done, re-ground through movement and awareness of the Earth.

- **Mandala** with chalk pastel or paint
Continue expressing the meditation energy within the circle of your mandala.

- **Free write.**

Channeling The Ones: Spirit

*We would say welcome to you on this morning...and we will speak on Spirit today, for it is in a sense, the culmination of the 7-chakra system. However, we understand that you know there are greater levels beyond this to which Spirit is connected. Here we are focused on who **you** are, the expression of **your** self in **this** incarnation. The Spirit is contained within the Soul - the Soul, we will speak on at a later time, contains or encompasses many expressions of Spirit. It is multidimensional in that sense, but today we will focus on Spirit itself and what makes you who **you** are, for when Spirit is born in this physical body, in this physical incarnation, you come through with certain intention of what it is you need to accomplish during your lifetime. The Spirit appears within the family unit which allows it certain experiences so that it may overcome certain limitations, overcome certain traumas, overcome its circumstances so that it may learn the lessons it is here to do. And then, oftentimes, that learning is connected to one's purpose here on Earth. And so, you might find yourself as a guide or a teacher for others who are experiencing the same. Then you can certainly see that you pave the way, open the pathway, if you will, for those who follow. This is if your issue or issues are resolved in the most positive way, for if in a sense your issue is unresolved or resolved, shall we say, negatively, unsuccessfully, the pattern repeats itself over and over again. However, if one goes deeply enough in one's inner process, to examine oneself you see, you can see the learning within. You can make sense of it in that way, so that it is resolved positively, and you overcome that experience to* *become a fuller expression of who you are. It is fairly simple – school exists on Earth, or Earth is a school, where these learning experiences take place, so that Spirit may evolve, yes, and return to the Soul in a more advanced level. When one is in touch with Spirit, you see there is a sense of enlivening, vitality, (inaudible) where there is little conflict, a lack of conflict, a sense of peace within, when you feel in alignment with who you truly are and what you're meant to be doing here on Earth. Yes…there's a sense of alignment, of peace and wellbeing. And so we would to encourage you to find that, to know yourself, to seek who you truly are in the most authentic way and let go of what is not you. This can be difficult when others put pressure on you to be something else than who you truly are. In a sense, you need to build that confidence in who you are so that you can stand tall in your own power. We will leave it there today, for as we continue our discussion, we will speak more broadly about Soul and its connection with All That Is. And so go in peace and enjoy the day.*

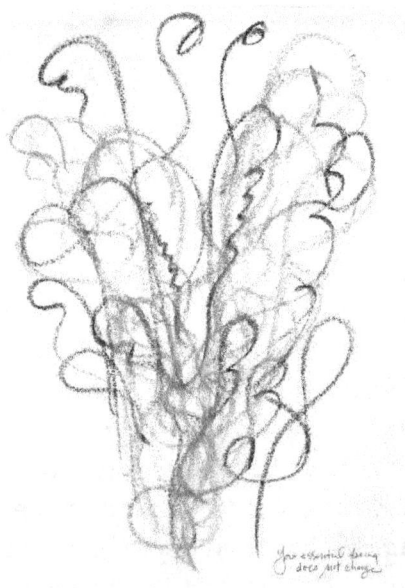

Your essential being does not change

Chapter 10
The Higher Chakras

We often think of the chakras existing only within the body, extending from the root at the base of the spine to the crown at the top of the head. But the reality is that it's a more complex system than that. There's the Earthstar chakra beneath, and several others above and behind the head. I'm going to stick with what I know here; not what others say – as I said, this book is based on my knowledge and experience. Others will have more to add.

There is, about four inches above the head, the Soul Star chakra (*Vyapini*). Imagine a ball of brilliant white light. This is your connection with Soul, a higher level of awareness. And again, the gateway to higher realms. My feeling is, once the Crown chakra is open, we have access to these higher aspects of ourselves, simply by putting our attention here. We can go even higher. By imagining a spinning silver disc, we can reach the Galactic Chakra, about seven to ten inches above the head, which allows us to communicate with other beings of light. I channeled Ashtar and the Pleiadians many years ago from this level. And above that, at twelve to fourteen inches above the head, is a seventh dimensional energy, which I associate with the angelic realm. I've heard it referred to as the Godhead Chakra. The experience is very high and very sweet; when channeling this, my voice is altered. I am able to channel for others here, perceiving what I would not be able to perceive in an "ordinary" channeling state or trance.

The Merkabah appeared to me automatically in meditation, along with information on its crystalline nature as a vehicle for reaching higher realms. This was presented to me by Metatron for the work with the energy wheels or mandalas I'd be painting. I believe, however, that by imagining that upward triangle of the Merkabah's shape and putting focus at the top of the triangle where activation occurs, you can travel upwards. Once you clear the Crown, you're on your way. My experience of this is very high and I am totally absorbed. By reversing the process, imagining the downward pointing triangle, you will re-ground.

I am not being asked to offer expressive arts experiences for these higher chakras. They are accessed through meditation. You can then use painting or drawing, dancing, or making music to ground those energies, and to make them visible – put them into form. I feel this is what I was instructed to do when I did the twelve *Sacred Geometry* mandalas. It's one thing to experience them, and another to ground those frequencies in order to facilitate the elevation of our planetary consciousness, or to make them visible so that people start to realize they exist. We are not just this physical body, we are not just this energetic body; we are aspects of the Divine, and we have a communication system to connect with That. We are not separate from it – it is Us. We are One. To some this may sound fantastic, especially those who are still focused on living through the physical. But there are enough of us now on the planet who are perceiving and interacting with these frequencies, here to boost not only the energy of humanity and Earth, but to elevate our awareness of their existence. Once that expansion of awareness exists, change or transformation on a global and Universal level can manifest.

Channeling the Ones: Soul Star

*We speak to you from the perspective of what you identify as the Soul Star, the energy center which is above the head, which is often depicted in your art as the halo, the light above and behind the head. Yes? It is often painted in these works of art as radio signals, which you do not perceive. This is the communication center. In fact, there is more than one, because as you rise higher you encounter stronger signals coming from the galactic center. And so there you might communicate with beings of...higher dimensions. The place above the head which we identify as the Soul Star is a wordless place, a place of divine bliss, pure energy...but in fact, one can travel using that Merkabah, to realms beyond even that. It is a transportation vehicle. The topmost point of your Merkabah activates the system. You can travel beyond the stars... It is your connection to All That Is, whatever terms you use to describe That Essence. There's not much need to speak on this center for it is simply something to be experienced through your devotional or meditative practices by raising your attention to this level... Therefore, we would encourage you to pick up such a practice within your routine, in your life, so that you can also experience that level of awareness... It is not something that you can take for granted – it is something needed to be experienced on an individual level, though within that context, within that connection, you see, you feel you are a part of All That Is. The boundary, in that sense, is dissolved. You are a soul within an oversoul, within the galactic consciousness, within the Universal consciousness, and so it expands... In order to make sense of this, one can drop the energy into the heart center and incorporate it into one's ordinary consciousness, into one's ordinary life. And so we would actually encourage people to **ground** the energy as you are now going through this planetary change, yes, both individually and collectively, as the channel has spoken of. Putting this highest – we will repeat that – **highest** level energy into form will bring that new planetary experience into manifestation. Since you are a piece of that whole, your personal expression is crucial in this process in order to achieve that wholeness. You are not separate from it. Many people perceive the, shall we say Godhead, or highest consciousness as something separate from them, outside of them. And yet we say it is You – your essence. Seek that within. Rise higher in your awareness and then it is your fulfillment to bring it into physicality, into manifestation. That will create the new* *world. We are honored to have supported this project as it has been revealed and congratulate you, every one of you, on your participation in this evolutionary experience. We are the Guides, the Ones, and send you our blessings.*

Energy of the Universe Activated   Nancy Winternight

Chapter 11
Manifesting Our NEW Reality

You will find joy in the newness.

~ The Ones

I was born with the initials NEW (Nancy Ellen White). My maternal grandmother, Rose, chose this name for me. As a child it seemed interesting, even significant, that my initials spelled out a real word, unlike most people's. As I moved into adulthood and a conscious spirituality, I began to understand its significance more meaningfully. I have always embraced change. I love creating and re-creating as I move through various cycles of my life; even each new moon brings an opportunity for renewal. Each *moment* brings opportunity for beginning anew. In this life, at this time, as we move into the Aquarian Age, grounding the values of peace, love, light, and Oneness, I am one of those people among many whose mission is to facilitate this change in dimension, ushering in a higher level of awareness for humanity and for the planet Earth.

As I'm writing this, the Earth is consumed in fires and floods. We call it climate change. There's also a lot of distress and rage, divisiveness, and blame. But understand that we are collectively co-creators. As we come into humanity's adulthood - our autonomy, as we realize that we are responsible for our personal states of being, as well as our effect on the collective, we must face our personal inner turmoil, our personal distress, our personal rage, our personal blame. **We** are co-creating the state of the planet, not some unseen force. It's us. The only way we can alter this reality is to do the real emotional and spiritual work. We need to ***transmute*** our challenging emotional energy into what will heal ourselves and, ultimately, the planet through the collective. We've heard the call to awaken – healing begins on the individual level; it impacts those around us whether we do the work or not, but it's our choice whether that impact is positive or not.

Expressive arts present an accessible tool for this ***alchemy***, the transmutation of emotion into healing energy and greater awareness. It's time to stop burying it, stop denying it. Earth is responding to it. Let's do ourselves and the Earth a favor and expand into a higher, more peaceful state of being.

Recently, I was baking my son-law-law, Sean, a pie for his birthday. The crust wasn't entirely circular, and I had to patch it a bit. And then, being a perfectionist, I wanted the lattice work on the top crust to be just right. If the dough didn't behave, I could *feel* myself tensing up. That's my pattern. Instead, I said, "I love you, pie." Instantly, my body relaxed, my experience altered, and joy seeped in. This was an 'aha' moment for me. This simple change in my energy – within my control, altered not only what I was feeling, but what I was releasing into my atmosphere (and into the pie). I could change my attitude in a moment, simply by saying those words: *I love you, pie.* I've decided that this will be my new strategy in this new time. As soon as I become aware of being stressed, I will say, *I love you, computer, I love you, traffic, I love you, so-and-so*. I can say it to them at a Soul level. We've heard that change begins at home. Well, here it is. I take responsibility for my own well-being and the well-being of my piece of the collective Pie. Together, we can choose to co-create a new reality. *I love you, Pie.*

Channeling the Ones

We understand that these are enormous leaps of consciousness, from one moment to the next, at least seemingly so, which can feel unsettling, as if the ground beneath you is moving, shifting. We assure you, you are grounded in consciousness. This is not a disappearing act, you see. But what we wish you to understand is that there is purest potential, purest perfection, in any one moment. In any one moment is pure perfection, so all that is necessary for you is to tune into that moment, and all is perfectly well. Go there to find the sense of security you all seek, that stability, that protection you all seek. By going within in any one moment you find that. That is all we wish to say, for today. Go in peace and enjoy the day.

There really is little else to add, dear ones, for you have heard the news – life on Earth is new from this time forward. Continuing to live in the past, according to old patterns and beliefs will only cause distress to you, and lower your energy, deplete your vitality. Renew yourselves from the inside out, and you will begin to see the results all around you. Perhaps it takes a level of faith to make this leap, yes? But we know that deep within you, you know this is why you're here now. The powers within your media talk far too much to distract you – the truth does not exist outside yourselves. What you see there is a reflection of your inner worlds, your inner collective world. Remember it is a PROCESS of change, a process of transformation, and though it seems as if it is taking forever, it is happening in the blink of an eye. You can see yourselves, you are no longer who you were a year or two ago. If you are trying to be, then you've caused yourself undue distress. We wish only blessings of newness for you, as we move into this expansive, rebirth of Earth. Cross that threshold and know peace. We love you at the deepest level. Know this to be true.

~The Ones who are in Service to All.

Julia, MC, Kara, Rita, Kloe, and Lauryn painting what they have to offer our new world: *Empathy, compassion, understanding*, and *peace*... They are so absorbed, they don't speak a word.

Author's Note

I thank those close to me who support me unconditionally as Who I Am, and I thank my Guides, the Ones, as well as my angelic and spirit guides who are always there for me, whenever I go within, open, and attune (and even when I don't).

Starry Winternight   Nancy Winternight   Photo credit: Juda Leah

Nancy Winternight is an artist, teacher, spiritual counselor, and intuitive living just outside of the infamous Woodstock, New York. She teaches Expressive Arts and offers both group and private sessions for those exploring a new way of being and co-creation of a new Earth. She is the author of *Soul Map: Channeling, Art, and Self-Realization.*

For more information, visit her website: www.nancywinternight.com.

Cover art: Nancy Winternight, *Creativity*, 12" x 12" acrylic on canvas.
Back cover art: Theresa Figueroa